D1473894

JAN 21 1966

GROWING UP IN CITIES:
Studies of the Spatial Environment
of Adolescence in Cracow, Melbourne, Mexico City,
Salta, Toluca, and Warszawa

Edited by Kevin Lynch

From the Reports of Tridib Banerjee,
Antonio Battro and Eduardo Ellis, Peter Downton,
Maria Susułowska and Tadeusz Tomaszewski

The MIT Press
Cambridge, Massachusetts, and London, England
UNESCO, Paris

© UNESCO 1977

Published jointly by the United Nations Educational, Scientific and Cultural Organization, 7 Place de Fontenoy, Paris 75700, France, and The Massachusetts Institute of Technology.

All rights reserved. No part of this book may be reproduced in any form or by any means, electronic or mechanical, including photocopying, recording, or by any information storage and retrieval system, without permission in writing from the publisher.

This book was set in IBM Composer Press Roman by Margaret Hayman, and printed and bound by Murray Printing Company in the United States of America.

Library of Congress Cataloging in Publication Data
Main entry under title:

Growing up in cities.

    Bibliography: p.
    1. City children—Case studies. 2. Personal space—Case studies. 3. Geographical perception—Case studies. 4. Children—Attitudes—Case studies.
I. Lynch, Kevin. II. Banerjee, Tridib.
HT206.G76   301.43'14   77-6789
ISBN 0-262-12078-X (M.I.T. Press)
ISBN 92-3-101443-9 (UNESCO)

CONTENTS

UNESCO FOREWORD

Discovering how people live today is a major concern for laymen, planners, and those members of public and administrative bodies whose work is concerned with improving the quality of life in cities, towns, and villages throughout the world. People continue to move to towns and cities. Urbanization often involves hardships and sometimes it is the young who have the heaviest burden of all to bear.

This book adopts an angle of approach which tends to be overlooked: How do children and adolescents themselves feel about "growing up in cities"? They are both the youngsters of today and the adults who will face the problem from the other side of the generation divide tomorrow.

Their subjective perception of the environment they live in, just as, in a wider perspective, that of all dwellers in towns and cities, has to be assessed as an important factor in attempts to make a better quality of life a reality for all.

This task has, of course, been taken up by the United Nations. UNESCO is operating an intergovernmental "Man and the Biosphere" programme which is investigating environmental perception as a major item of research in cooperation with social scientists of all nations.

These studies represent another step in the long learning process necessary to ensure its amelioration of living conditions so urgently necessary for so many people in our modern world. The opinions expressed, however, are those of the editor and other contributors, and do not necessarily reflect those of UNESCO.

GROWING UP IN CITIES

GROWING UP IN CITIES

Under UNESCO sponsorship, research teams in Argentina, Australia, Mexico, and Poland have looked at the way small groups of young adolescents use and value their spatial environment. This report recommends that these studies, with some modifications, be extended in a number of countries in a long range program of international research.

The intention of these first studies was "to help document the human costs and benefits of economic development, by showing how the child's use and perception of the resulting micro-environment affects his life." The research was meant to suggest public policies for improving the spatial environment. In the process, we hoped that we might learn some things about environmental indicators, long-term changes in child environment, the misperceptions of planners and educators, and the latent public support for improvement. Finally, these efforts were to show how international support could build local research interest and capability, which in its turn would inform local and national policy.

The small size of these studies, the varied conditions under which they were conducted, and the necessary modifications of the research method, all preclude rigorous comparisons or broad generalizations between them. This was predicted in the original guidelines.

But some impressions have emerged. These studies can be completed using very simple means, and they produce information relevant to local planning decisions. The techniques are easily modified to fit local conditions and priorities. They can initiate further policy-linked research, and develop local research teams in the process. Building local capability brings such knowledge to bear on public actions.

Even these few studies bring out poignant indications of the relations of children to their surroundings.

In doing so, they convey the color and substance of social conditions that are usually summarized in a more arid and general form. However uncertain the findings may yet be, they reverberate in the mind, and suggest new techniques and new occasions. Open-ended, naturalistic studies of how people use and value their spatial surroundings are in an early stage. The values of children have been particularly neglected.

The original guidelines under which the first investigations were conducted are reproduced on pages 99-104. In brief, they called for interviews with a group of twenty children in early adolescence, all living in one locality. They were to be asked how they used, conceived of, and felt about their surroundings. Investigators were to observe how the children actually used the setting, make a careful physical description of the place, and conduct comparative interviews with parents and with officials concerned with the public planning of the locality.

Studies in Four Nations

The studies have been carried out in Argentina and Australia, in two locations in Mexico, and in several locations in Poland. While the original intent was to emphasize the settlements of the in-migrant poor (those persons presumably most exposed to environmental stress) the first investigations, except for one colonia in Mexico, have been of relatively stable settlements of farmers, the working class, or the lower middle class. Most of these people were living in relatively developed nations. These studies serve as examples of method, and as a probe of its strength and weakness; we hope that future studies will turn more often to those areas and nations with even more critical problems.

The Argentinian study by Dr. Antonio Battro and architect Eduardo Ellis looked at a small, well-defined

community (Las Rosas) on the outskirts of the provincial city of Salta in northern Argentina. Peter
Downton's research dealt with a larger and more
amorphous portion of the western suburbs of the city
of Melbourne in Australia. Profs. Tadeusz Tomaszewski and Maria Susułowska, research psychologists in
Warszawa and Cracow, made comparative studies of
two inner-city locations (Powisle and Kleparski), two
peripheral housing projects (Zatrasie and Kozłowka),
and a rural village (Bystra Podhalanska). Dr. Tridib
Banerjee conducted an analysis of a neighborhood in
Toluca (Colonia Universidad), the provincial capital
of the State of Mexico, and another in Ecatepec
(Colonia San Agustin), a largely self-built housing
settlement about 16 kilometers north of Mexico City,
just at the latest front of metropolitan expansion.
These studies are excellently described in the original
reports. We have summarized those reports in a free,
impressionistic way and suggest a revised set of methods and aims for a longer-term program of international research.

Salta

As different as these locations are in their geography and culture, there are parallels between them. The
Argentine and Australian cases are areas of single-
family houses built by the government for low- or
moderate-income families in the 1950s. Both areas
reflect the unanticipated costs and benefits, to children, of the way government moved to meet the
housing problem a generation ago. Two of the Polish
examples are large apartment house projects built
within the last few years and may be contrasted to
two other areas of crowded, prewar flats at the very
edge of the city center.

Melbourne

The study areas differ sharply in other ways. They
vary in climate and landscape: a mountain-ringed valley, deep within a continent; a flat, rather dry plain
close to the edge of a shallow ocean bay; a humid,
wooded agricultural region lying along the course of a

Warsaw
Cracow
Bystra

Ecatepec
Toluca

1
The entrance to the
community of Las
Rosas in the city of
Salta, Argentina.
(See pages 120-123,
and Figs. 19, 25, 57,
and 58)

2
The western suburbs
of Melbourne: small
wooden houses along
the unplanted streets.
(See pages 105-108,
and Figs. 14, 18, 24,
26, 49, and 55)

3
Small houses and
barren parks in
Melbourne.

4
Looking out over the central city neighborhood of Powisle in Warsaw: new apartments and prewar housing bisected by elevated bridge approaches. The Vistula is to the left, the city center is on the escarpment to the right and behind. (See pages 149-150)

5
Old and new flats in crowded Powisle.

6
Kleparski market
square at the edge of
old Cracow, looking
away from the central
city. (See pages 133-
134)

7
A general view of the
edge of the new resi-
dential quarter of
Zatrasie. The Palace
of Culture, at the
center of Warsaw,
shows dimly in the
distance. (See page
150 and Fig. 20)

8
The new quarter of
Kozłowka on the
periphery of Cracow.
(See pages 134-136,
and Fig. 21)

9
The rural setting of
Bystra Podhalanska.
(See pages 136-137,
and Fig. 22)

10
Aerial view of
Colonia Universidad
in Toluca, Mexico.
(See pages 154-155,
and Figs. 16 and 17)

11
A typical street in
Colonia Universidad:
blank walls, utility
poles, new pavements.

12
A typical street in
Colonia San Agustin,
Ecatepec, Mexico—the
residents are still
building. (See page
161 and Figs. 15 and
27)

13
The main shopping
street of the colonia
in Ecatepec.

historic, major river; a harsh, arid flat with alkaline soil and little plant life on a former lake bed. Three settlements are Latin American in culture, another Anglo-American, the other Slavic. Salta is a historic, provincial city of moderate size in an economically depressed region of Argentina. Toluca is a similar provincial city, with its own identity; it is much smaller but is now growing. Cracow is a historic center of 600,000 people, a city of ancient lineage still blessed with an active economy. Its residents would be annoyed to be called provincial. Melbourne is a large, rapidly growing Australian metropolis. Ecatepec is at the extreme edge of Mexico City, which is growing explosively. Warszawa is much smaller, yet it is the national capital. The Argentine community has an exceptionally well-defined physical setting, backed by low open hills. The Australian area is one piece of an extensive, somewhat characterless, single-family suburban region. Colonia Universidad, in a newly developing part of Toluca, has undergone dramatic transformations in the last four or five years, during which utilities and paving have been installed and some apartments added to the original single-family stock. Colonia San Agustin, in Ecatepec, is still a partly makeshift single-family area surrounded by dry and dusty wastelands. Electricity and water run along most of its streets, but many of them are still unpaved. The Polish housing projects, built in the mass apartment housing style seen everywhere today, are in the amorphous outskirts of their cities; the inner settlements are a mix of old and new flat buildings and commerce, deafened by the center city bustle at their doorsteps. The village in the foothills of the Tatra Mountains (Bystra Podhalanska), although now part of the industrial economy, is rural and quiet.

The Australians are working class people with incomes well below the national median. Many of them are refugees of World War II and settled in Melbourne a generation ago. The residents of San Agustin are poor, rural migrants, drawn from a wide radius by the glamor and work opportunities of the big city. San Augustin is the second step in their migration, the first step being the crowded vecindades of the center city where two-thirds of the family heads still work as laborers or in casual occupations. The people in Colonia Universidad in Toluca are a more stable group; most are originally from Toluca and its vicinity, and while many are still on the lower end of the income scale, some are approaching the lower middle class. The Argentines are more nearly lower middle class, with incomes somewhat above the median. They are mixed in occupation and status but are often employed in local government. Their houses are appreciably better than the self-built housing to the west, toward the city center. While some of these Argentine families came from rural areas, most moved in from other locations in the city. The urban Poles are mixed in occupation but are primarily working class. They are recent arrivals in the housing projects. The village people have long roots in their locality but are now beginning to desert it for the city. Finally, it appears from these studies that the Argentine community is coherent and stable, animated by hope despite the problems it may endure. The Polish villagers, members of a strong, traditional rural society, are undergoing a very rapid—and to them hopeful—social change. The city people, whose communities are far less coherent, are seeing changes too; however, judging from their children, their view of the future is less optimistic. In Melbourne people think of themselves as being at the bottom of society, even though their way of life in material terms is substantially higher than that in Salta, Mexico, or Poland. If these Australians have hopes for themselves or their children, it is to be somebody else and to get away.

These differences generate expectable differences
in our results. But the gulf makes certain similarities
in the data all the more remarkable. It is probably
true that comparative studies sufficiently accurate to
be useful for policy decisions will have to be conducted within a single culture, comparing variances in
single factors of class, age, or environment. Policy
makers are well advised to suspect findings imported
from other nations. Yet the similarities we find in
these disparate cases indicate the possibility of some
human constants in the way children use their world.
Moreover, it is clear that the same techniques of observation, barring a few necessary minor modifications, were useful in these diverse places.

The research teams, while carrying through the indicated procedures, were stimulated to branch out in
studies of their own. Battro and Ellis supplemented
their investigation with Piagetian analyses of the mental structure of the environmental image, with free
discussions while engaged in a city walk and while
standing on a hilltop overlooking Salta, and with an
interesting attempt to encourage the children to generate their own ideas for environmental improvement.
Downton developed new ways of observing street behavior when it was extremely mobile and wide ranging, and related his study results to pressing policy
issues in the Melbourne region. The Mexican interview schedules were somewhat truncated and modified; and the interviews with parents and professionals
were substantially eliminated. On the other hand, new
techniques were used, such as employing photographs
to elicit responses. Additional questions relating to
sex differences and aspirations were asked, and an
analysis of house form was made in Ecatepec. The
Mexican interviews were carried out by non-natives
for whom Spanish was a second language; however,
the interviewers felt that they had good rapport with
the children and that they received candid answers

despite the barriers of culture and language. The studies have generated much interest in Mexico and follow-ups in four other sites of varying climate are being considered. The Polish group made a fascinating analysis of the combined effects of variations in environment and individual psychological makeup, and may now branch out to study the spatial settings of the elderly. We hope that this local initiative will continue. Standardization for the sake of comparison is important, but the fit to local requirements is paramount.

What follows is not a rigorous comparison. We have already explained why such a comparison is not possible. Nevertheless, some of the interesting differences and similarities between these places will give a sense of the data that can be produced. The reader should refer to the reports themselves. They are not the usual appendixes of footnotes, detailed method, or raw data. They are independent studies.

The Use of Unprogrammed Space

There are similarities in the way these thirteen- and fourteen-year-olds use the "unprogrammed" spaces near their dwellings: the local streets, the courtyards, the apartment staircases. They talk and meet and walk about together, they play informal pick-up games, they "mess around," as the Australians would say, in a seemingly aimless fashion, which to their parents often appears, not .wrong, but idle. (Indeed, there are indications that the investigators themselves were at times a little disapproving.) Just beginning to assert their independence of the family, they are testing a society of their own, and the street is the place for it. Streets are immediately at hand, and it is legitimate to be in them. Interesting things happen in the streets, and yet street behavior is not rigidly prescribed. In Ecatepec and the Polish center cities in

14
Everything happens
on the street in
Melbourne.

15
Streets and vacant
lots are the play-
grounds of Ecatepec.

particular, the street is an important extension of the crowded home.

When asked about what they choose to do, the places they are interested in, how they spend their time, or how they would like to, the children do not talk much about school, the playground, or even their own private yards. They talk about the street or courtyard, their own room if they have one, and, to a lesser degree, the sports facilities, the wastelands, the natural open spaces, and the center of the city. There are some interesting exceptions to this rule. One is that the children of Ecatepec speak frequently of their school; it appears prominently on their maps. The other exception is that the Tolucan children mention the streets much less often in describing their activities. Clearly, they are intimidated by the overbearing traffic that pours through their neighborhood. The streets themselves have no nooks or crannies; the sidewalks are narrow and lined with unrecessed facades and fences. The traffic pavements are patently dangerous. Thus, the children turn to the formal parks and playgrounds of the city, which fortunately are within their reach. The diagrams and photographs of activity from Melbourne, on the other hand, contrast their free use of streets and waste places (or of a casual meeting place such as the front stoop of the squash court building) with the programmed use—indeed, mostly the emptiness—of the playgrounds and reserves. Unfortunately, neither the Polish nor the Argentine teams were able to carry out a similar field recording of activity, and yet their photographs show the Las Rosas children using their streets and the Zatrasie and Kozłowka children using their courtyards in much the same way. The shape of the local streets, stairs, and courtyards is important to these children: the paving, the trees, the safety, the suitability for informal play, the corners, doorways, nooks, and benches where they can meet their

16
Street play is
dangerous in Toluca.

17
And so one finds the
children in the formal
park in the center of
the colonia.

18
Passing the time on
the steps of the squash
courts building in
Melbourne.

19
Using the streets of
Las Rosas.

20
A playground in
Zatrasie.

21
And another in
Kozłowka.

22
The school yard
in Bystra.

Weekday Distribution of Activity	0600	0700	0800	0900	1000	1100	1200	1300	1400	1500	1600	1700	1800	1900	2000	2100	2200	2300	2400
awake	:	:	::	::											.	:	. .	.	
ablutions	.	:	::	:::															
breakfast		:	::	:::															
attending younger siblings			:	:	.														
household chores			.	::	:							.	:	:	:	.	:		
journey to school				:	::	:													
school classes					:::::	:::::	:::::	:::::	:::::	:::::							.		
other school (incl. school-organized sport)				.	.				::::										
journey home											:::::	:	:	:					
homework											::	::	::	.	:	:	:	. .	.
organized youth activities and other lessons												.	.	.	:	.	. .		
working											.	:	:	.	.	.	. .	.	.
shopping											:	:	.		.				
interaction with relatives	/														. .	. .	. .	.	
interaction with friends adjacent to house											:	.	.						
visiting friends			.	:							.	:	::	:	:	.	:	:::	.
sport (incl. organized sport, informal sport, and minibiking)											.	.	. .	.		:	:	:	
messing around outdoors												.	.	.	:	.	.	.	
messing around indoors				:								.	.	.					
reading			.									.	:		: .	: .	. :	. .	. :
hobbies											.	.	.	:	:	:	.		
watching televison			.								.	.	::	:::	:::	:::	:::::	:::::	:
evening meal													:	::	::				
bed time																:	:::	:	.

23
Activities of twenty
Melbourne children
on a weekday by
half-hour intervals:
an example of a time
chart. (Skeptical
readers may amuse
themselves by finding
minor discrepancies
in these data.)

friends, the opportunities those places give them to slip away from the parental eye while still being thought safe and under general supervision.

Time Budgets

Looking at the time budgets, one is struck by the rigidity of the weekday—school in the morning and early afternoon, then homework (for some), then the television. Unlike their parents in their day, these children (except for the rural ones) are not doing paid labor or even many household chores. Yet there is little time when they freely organize their own activity—indeed, little time spent outdoors in any fashion. With 40 to 45 percent of their waking hours absorbed by school, homework, and other formal lessons, and 25 to 35 percent spent in meals, wash-ups, chores, and other maintenance (the higher figure for girls, the lower for boys), almost all remaining time is spent in front of the television set (or, in Ecatepec where there is no television, listening to the radio). Only 5 to 10 percent of their day is unprogrammed, and that time is spent on the streets, in their rooms, or at friends' houses. On the weekends school time almost disappears, outdoor activity climbs to 25 to 40 percent, and unprogrammed time to 30 to 35 percent. This weekend free time is spent on the streets or in their rooms, and also in visits and outings. Unfortunately, the comprehensive Polish time budget data is unclear, but it appears that a child's play in Poland is also heavily scheduled. In contrast to the other countries, even the weekends are fully organized and under adult control. This is even more marked in the village where children have substantial chores to do and a heavier school load as well. Thus, village children have almost no "idle" time. The Mexican girls also have an important role in household maintenance: cooking, washing, feeding

"They just hang around the street and there's nothing for them to do. That's no way to bring up kids!" *Melbourne*

"I usually get up at six o'clock. I tidy the flat, light the stove. When I come back from school, I have dinner and do homework and then I sew or embroider. Sometimes I meet my friends for an hour. At half past five I prepare food for the cattle and feed them. This usually takes until seven. Then I have supper, and watch the "goodnight" program and a film, if it is one I am allowed to." *Bystra*

"I always have to be home around one-thirty. I come from La Villa and the bus is sometimes slow. And if I arrive late, I have to explain to my mother why I'm late—because I went to buy a book or something. And my mama knows if I'm telling the truth or not. And she either hits me or she doesn't. Afterwards, I help her with what she needs to do. But there are times when I don't help her and she gets mad at me. Because sometimes I'm tired, or I have to study, or I'm being lazy! During the week I don't help her at all, because I go to classes, then have to study all afternoon. I don't do anything besides doing the dishes and cleaning the table and study all day. It's that at school the teachers don't give us vacations. If we don't do our homework they call our parents. . . ."
Ecatepec

the animals, gathering firewood, attending younger brothers and sisters, marketing, running errands, feeding adult members of the family. In fewer cases, the Mexican children contribute to family production: helping a carpenter father, attending the store, making paper flowers and delivering them downtown.

The Polish team also compared the hours devoted to sleep and play by children whose temperaments required either a high or a low level of stimulus, and who lived either in noisy, active Powisle, or quiet, isolated Zatrasie. Thus the temperaments of two groups (the high stimulus seekers in Powisle, and the low stimulus seekers in Zatrasie) were presumably better matched to the character of their settings than were the other two. The analysts found that the percentage of time spent in sleep and play by children who were "adapted" to active Powisle was very close to the general average, while those "adapted" to quiet Zatrasie devoted less time to either activity. The "understimulated"—the high stimulus seekers living in Zatrasie, the quiet periphery—slept much longer than the others, but played about the same length of time, while the "overstimulated"—the lovers of calm in noisy Powisle—spent more time at play yet slept the normal period. Extra time for play or sleep was taken from the time allotted for homework, but average school grades were unaffected. So much for homework!

The Range of Action

The Salta children play within part of a circle which is only 1/2 kilometer across. Their friends are close by. Some children do not even go as far as the small local plaza. They express confidence in moving anywhere within their city, but show less knowledge of it. They do know the center well, however. Since the Colonia Universidad streets are so inconvenient, even for "hanging out," the Tolucan children go to the city parks and the city center at least once a week and know them reasonably well. Children in the Polish housing projects keep consistently within their project bounds, which are only slightly larger than the Salta territory (1/4 to 1/2 square km). Their knowledge of the rest of the city was scattered and random. Their counterparts at the heart of Cracow and Warszawa roam the densely active central areas; their territories are more individualized and confident. The Ecatepec children fixed their action space in the nearby streets and their school. At the same time, they will spend an hour to an hour and a half in a crowded bus to travel to the center of Mexico City. They know its major elements: the subway, Chapultepec Park, the Zocalo, the Zona Rosa, and some even commute regularly. The Australians, however, are the most mobile, ranging over ground five square kilometers in extent, and occasionally much further. They are constantly on the move: walking, biking, riding. To visit a friend may mean a substantial trip. Indeed, judging from the numbers of cars, bikes, motor bikes, boats, and horses one sees in the street photographs, the emphasis on movement must be general. Despite this spatial range, the Australians seem to be exposed to a more restricted variety of people, activity, and place. They are less familiar with the center of their city (which is 13 km away compared to 2 km in Toluca, 3 km in Salta, 5 km in Kozłowka and Zatrasie, and 16 km in Ecatepec), and seemingly less at ease in traversing those sections of the metropolis that are unlike their own.

The important barriers to movement are not distance but personal fear, dangerous traffic, a lack of spatial knowledge, the cost of public transport, or, in case of the girls, parental controls. Girls are more often kept at home or must travel in pairs, while the boys are, at least in theory, free to roam. Some of the

Melbourne boys do so, but primarily within the western working class suburbs. The Tolucans and Saltese, who are within walking range, visit the center or the large parks but rarely travel elsewhere, despite their expressed freedom to do so. The children of Zatrasie and Kozłowka have relatively good public transport to the center, but complain of being cut off. The colonia in Ecatepec is truly isolated save for its public transport link—a long, crowded, and relatively expensive ride. The children have little understanding of their highly amorphous municipality, which is an archipelago of isolated colonias. "Opening" the entire city to these children—by means of transport, encouragement, or example—might be one way of educating them, strengthening their budding independence, and appeasing their hunger for stimulus.

Boredom and Engagement

The Melbourne children speak constantly of their boredom as do the children of Salta in a more muted way. There is little to do or see that is new. The children seem to suffer from experiential starvation. They are attracted to the sights of the center city or wait hungrily for something to happen. Even the research interviews were regarded as events to look forward to (although the research actually went unnoticed in the general community, as was intended). The Salta teenagers also enjoyed the novelty of the walks and the experiments. The Polish investigators speak of the hunger for activity and stimulus felt by the children in the outlying districts as a principal defect of these planned areas. In contrast, the center-city children, who are aware of their advantageous access to city excitement, are hungry for outdoor space in which to play. Feelings of boredom were less explicit in the Mexican responses, although to the adult researchers these colonias seemed exceedingly banal

"Nothing much. Just messing around; there's nothing else to do." *Melbourne*

"I like to be in the Old Town. I look at historic monuments. I like window-shopping." *Kozłowka*

"My street is the best to live in. It's in the center, you don't have to go anywhere by train." *Kleparski*

and unresponsive. Perhaps children's expectations are shaped by adult possibilities, which are so very limited in Toluca and Ecatepec.

In most of these settlements there is little for the children to be responsible for—no places they control and manage. The landscape is divided into ownerships (public or private) and the children are not the owners even though the vacant lots, the back lots, and the factory yards may not be actively used by anyone else. In Melbourne, the children were finally driven off the minibike track, the one bit of ground in all the area that they had changed to suit their own purposes. (The air photos show that previous tracks had been made and abandoned on other vacant lots. This must be a continuing guerrilla action.) Very few of the Polish city children speak of any place as "their own"; when they do, they are usually referring to a piece of furniture or, at most, part of a room. The case is different for the village children, however, half of whom refer to "their own" house, garden, or farmyard. Indeed, the children often share in the management of those places and thus, while working longer hours, are more explicitly connected to the community and the place. In a similar vein, the Las Rosas boys and girls often refer to their personal roles in the local nativity celebration.

Wastelands

The children are attracted to, and also somewhat fearful of, the waste grounds within their reach: the littered banks of the Maribyrnong River in Melbourne, or the scarred hills behind Las Rosas in Salta. Some of the children believe that the Las Rosas hills harbor "bad men" from the prison. The Bystra villagers imagine dangerous animals in their woods. The Maribyrnong is known to be rapid and polluted. Yet the Australians go through a screen of factories to

24
The pleasures of waste
ground, Melbourne.

25
The fearsome and
attractive hill behind
Las Rosas with its
grotto for the
nativity play.

26
The polluted
Maribyrnong valley is
an alluring place to
play.

explore that river, the Bystrans love their woods, the boys of Las Rosas play and seek solitude on their hills. The Tolucans have similar ambivalent feelings about the rocky hillsides on the north and west, and the volcano just outside the city; these wastelands are places of fascination, places where one can be alone and act independently.

Such feelings are not characteristic of Ecatepec, however. The children dislike and fear the vast expanses of the former lakebed surrounding the colonia. They dislike the trash that piles up there and the mud when it rains. They are afraid that they may fall into ditches or holes. They are afraid of the abandoned houses where there are drunks and robbers. They have no use for these salt flats—the one thing that is plentiful in their environment.

Interestingly enough, no comments on wastelands appear in the urban Polish data, although the peripheral projects, at least, have relatively empty lands nearby. Perhaps the parents do not allow their children to visit such places, or it is not proper to talk of such escapades. The great Vistula River, for one example, is readily accessible to the Powisle children, and yet it is curiously absent from their descriptions. True, it is separated from their apartments by a new and heavily traveled boulevard. It is certainly dangerous and fast flowing in flood. In any case, in the view of the Powisle children, the city center, above on the escarpment, is the much more important neighbor.

The Image of the Locality

A striking difference between the locales is the way in which the children image their community. Asked to draw a map of "the area you live in," the Salta children all draw the same coherent place. Villa Las Rosas is an area of similar houses, sharply bounded by a prison, the hills, and a main road with its canal.

27
A sterile, dried-up lake
bed surrounds the
colonia in Ecatepec.
The children avoid it.

It is neither richly equipped nor handsome, but it has a steel arch for an entrance, a dead-end main street for its axis, and a little central plaza. The two community facilities—church and school—are both on that axis, and the axis points to a grotto on the hills, the locale of an annual community celebration. The streets are all named for flowers. By climbing the hill just behind their settlement, the children can see it all laid out before them. By climbing a hill to the north, they can see the entire city in relation to the mountains and the farms.

Las Rosas is apparently not just a physical unit but an active community as well. It organizes a ten-day Christmas pageant which draws spectators from all of Salta. The children repeatedly mention their participation in the tableaux. On the hill, the neighbor's association is building a swimming pool; one or two of the boys helped clear the land for it. The children await its completion eagerly but impatiently since progress is slow. Most of the small, standard houses in the Villa have been added onto, and many of them boast decorated facades, elaborate front walls, and patterned sidewalks. (This public neatness contrasts with the house interiors, which are reported to be "heaped with objects.") Las Rosas has the appearance of a hopeful and active community, however meager its means. Physical and social identity seem to reinforce each other. Children play a small but recognizable part in community action.

"It is a nice area, many playful children. They play until late. The people are good. Many people go to the plaza at night. There are many birds in the hills." *Las Rosas*

Asked to describe their area, the Salta children repeatedly volunteer that it is "nice," friendly, protected, "fun." They talk of neighborhood friends and emphasize the Villa's trees (there are not really too many), its plaza, and its paved streets (in fact there are few). They say they prefer their own area to others in the city. They believe things will change for the better. Most of them expect to live in the Villa when they grow up. Some of these could be answers calculated to please the interviewer, but there is an undercurrent of consensus too strong to ignore. Standard houses, constructed according to a rather haphazard plan on an old garbage dump next to the penitentiary, have blossomed into a coherent society and place.

The drawings of the young Polish villagers are equally consistent. A main road parallels a stream, and along it are all the important institutions and activities of the village, which is closed in by woods and hills. The maps are crowded with vividly drawn outdoor activities and houses of friends. In fact, these maps exhibit over four times as many elements as those drawn by the children of central Cracow. There is a strong impression of a territory thoroughly known and personally participated in, a territory where the children are familiar with all the basic institutions of the community. Two-thirds of them say they intend to remain in the village when they grow up, although to judge from current trends they are quite mistaken. They say their village is changing rapidly (as it is), and changing for the better.

The neighborhood maps from the Zatrasie and Kozłowka housing projects give an utterly different impression. They are dominated by confused arrays of large dwelling blocks, most of them without any further detail or indication. Little is shown of anything beyond the project; thus, a consistent district is recorded, but one without a sense of boundary except for occasional major streets. These maps focus on the places with which the children are involved—primarily the outdoor play places between the blank ranges of apartments—and neglect most of the adult features. Although drawn in the winter, they are summertime maps. Attempts by Zatrasie children to convert their triangular area into a rectangle produce confusing results. Asked for drawings of the city as a whole, they produce "islands" of special activities

"The district where I live is called Bystra. There are big woods, and long fields where people work. There are pretty houses, some shops, a fine school, a fire station, and the parish library. Through the village winds a river, the Bystrzanka, which carries away bridges when there are floods. At harvest time the corn becomes golden. In winter everything is covered by snow. You can see boys skiing and sledding, and children playing." *Bystra*

"[Kozłowka] is a big estate and the communications with Cracow are not too bad. . . . Monotonous blocks, all grey. . . . It is still being developed." "This is chaos—a stranger can't find his way about. I would change the blocks— they look like barracks —so they wouldn't be all alike." *Kozłowka*

28
Two images of Las
Rosas: entrance arch,
chapel, religious
statue, tree-shaded
streets, and the hills
and the battlements
of the prison behind.
(Compare with the
photo of the actual
entrance, Fig. 1.)

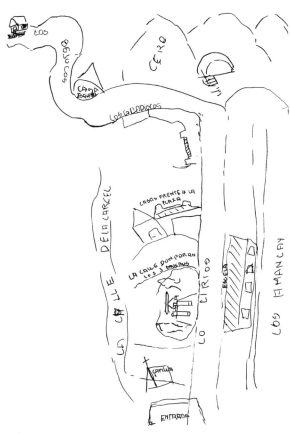

29
A twelve-year-old
girl's map of Las
Rosas: all the essen-
tial elements are in
place.

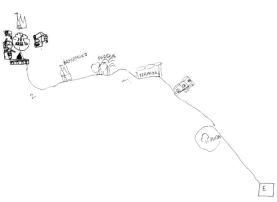

Her map of the whole
city is a journey to
the central plaza from
her school and local
plaza, marked by the
major landmarks along
the way.

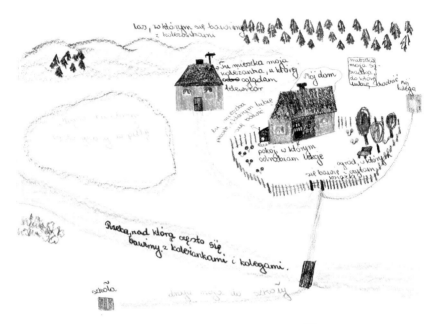

30
A home neighborhood
in Bystra (but much
of its quality is lost in
black and white!).

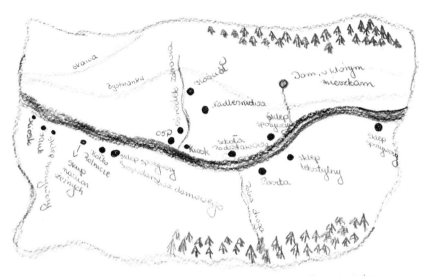

Bystra Podhalańska
Plan

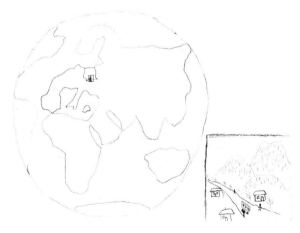

31
A child's plan of
Bystra Podhalanska:
the main road with all
its community facili-
ties, the stream, the
woods, and a
boundary.

32
Bystra's place in the
world.

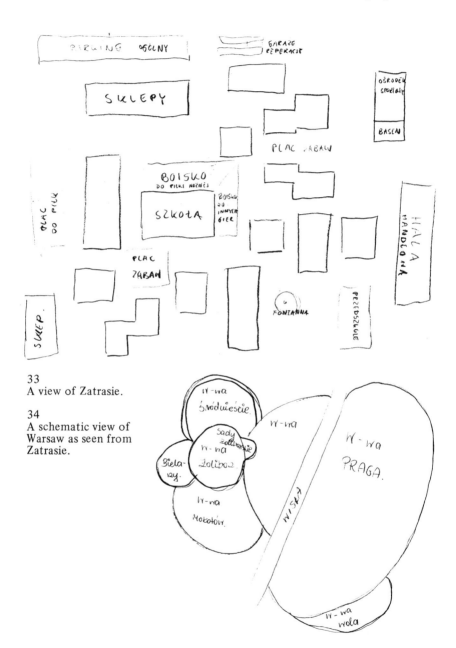

33
A view of Zatrasie.

34
A schematic view of
Warsaw as seen from
Zatrasie.

35
A plan of Kozłowka
and its repetitive
blocks.

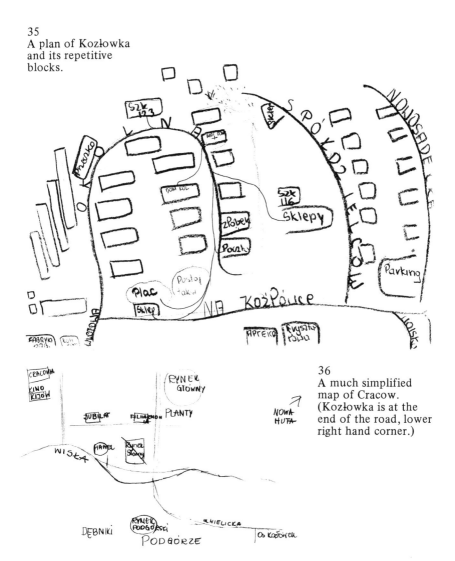

36
A much simplified
map of Cracow.
(Kozłowka is at the
end of the road, lower
right hand corner.)

"Nearby is a village, Praski Wielkie. It also neighbors Prokocim. It is different there, because there are not so many shops there and it is greener there. The houses are prettier and it's a bit cleaner than Kozłowka. The people are quite different and sort of better than Kozłowka people." *Kozłowka*

linked by long "bridges" of public transport. Less than half expect to continue to live where they are now. They are aware that the environment is constantly changing around them, but do not think of the change as an improvement. Of all the Polish children, they are the ones most critical of the places where they live (especially in Kozłowka), the most prone to think that good things are located elsewhere.

The central city children in Poland, on the other hand, produce much more systematic and accurate maps based on elaborate street networks and filled with shops, institutions, places of entertainment, and historical memorials. They are more diverse in the area they cover and the elements they contain. They have a place of their own (Kleparski square in the one case, or Tamka Street and its crossings in the other), but it is seen as lying at the edge of a familiar and active center. If asked to make maps of the whole city, they simply turn their attention more fully to that center and do not go beyond it. The knowledge of central Warszawa is not as impressive or as saturated with history as that of central Cracow, but both groups of children know the adult city as well as the locales most useful to them. They find their own area interesting, spend much time walking the streets, and often discover new places. Nearly all of them expect to live there in the future. Still, it is a dangerous place (the traffic, the "hooligans," and drunks), and it is noisy and dirty. Their dwellings are cramped and there is little place to play. They would like to see the area change, but fear it will not, or that it will change for the worse—parking garages may take over the small, open spaces, for example.

One additional test further illuminated the differences between adolescent lives in central and peripheral Warszawa. The children were asked to list the people they knew, then to mark what the relationship was (neighbor, relative, etc.), and how often and where they met; the children were finally to scale how they evaluated those connections (as friendly, useful, etc., or the reverse). The center city (Powisle) children knew more people than the suburban (Zatrasie) children, but fewer were relatives, neighbors, or schoolmates. Their contacts were to a larger degree temporary or occasional and more often neutrally, or even negatively, valued.

Colonia Universidad in Toluca is almost solidly residential—a regular, rectangular grid sharply bounded by arterial streets and a huge athletic field. The children's maps are accurate street maps with a few pictorial embellishments—the church, school, and scattered shops, which stand out in that relatively featureless setting. These maps give the sense of a corridor world, completely defined by unbroken, low facades. Doors are the important features. The recent paving and lighting of those corridors was a striking and welcome event.

While Toluca is a relatively small, compact city whose edge is easily discernible and streets reasonably well structured, most of these children cannot represent it. A third of them could not, or would not, draw a city map. Others simply extended the area of their own colonia somewhat. Most made vivid, pictorial representations of the central plaza and its distinctive buildings. They are well acquainted with that center, with the major city parks, and with the hills and volcano outside the city. But the few who tried to draw the entire city floundered unsuccessfully among various strategies of integration.

In the much larger Colonia San Agustin of Ecatepec, the main streets run east-west. The north-south streets, narrowed by encroachments, serve only as connectors. Most stores are on Avenida Lourdes, the east-west spine. The sections settled first have houses with outside plaster work and painting—some even have private gardens and gates. The streets here are cleaner. Toward the periphery, the houses turn to

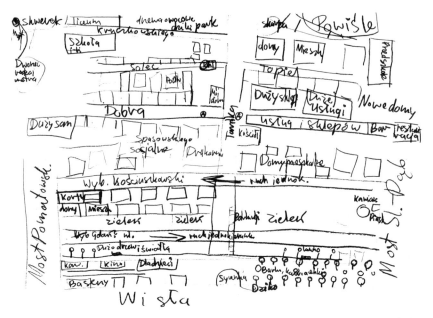

37
The dense and active
Powisle quarter.

38
The very center of
Warsaw is immediate-
ly above Powisle and
its Tamka Street.
(Compare this map of
Warsaw with Figure
34.)

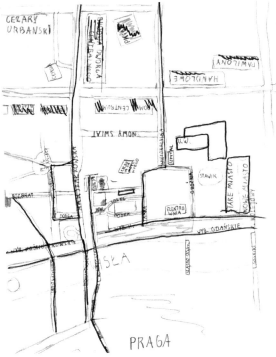

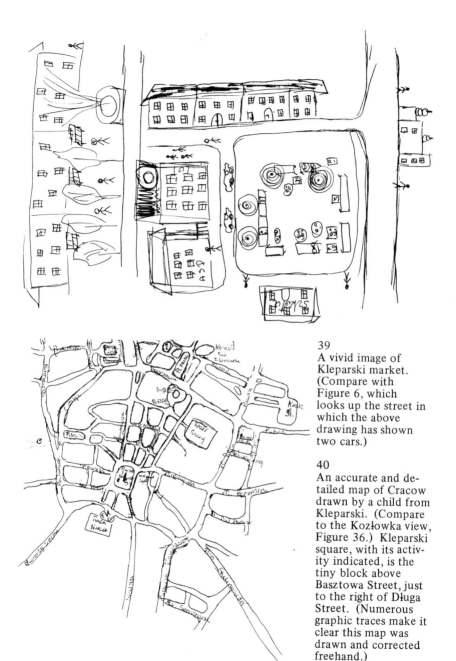

39
A vivid image of
Kleparski market.
(Compare with
Figure 6, which
looks up the street in
which the above
drawing has shown
two cars.)

40
An accurate and de-
tailed map of Cracow
drawn by a child from
Kleparski. (Compare
to the Kozłowka view,
Figure 36.) Kleparski
square, with its activ-
ity indicated, is the
tiny block above
Basztowa Street, just
to the right of Długa
Street. (Numerous
graphic traces make it
clear this map was
drawn and corrected
freehand.)

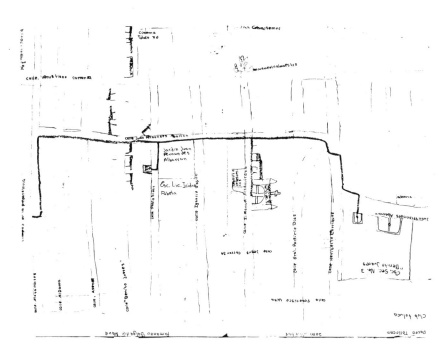

41
Two views of Colonia
Universidad in
Toluca—a world of
corridor streets,
doors, and house-
fronts.

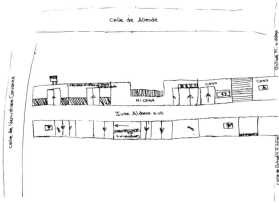

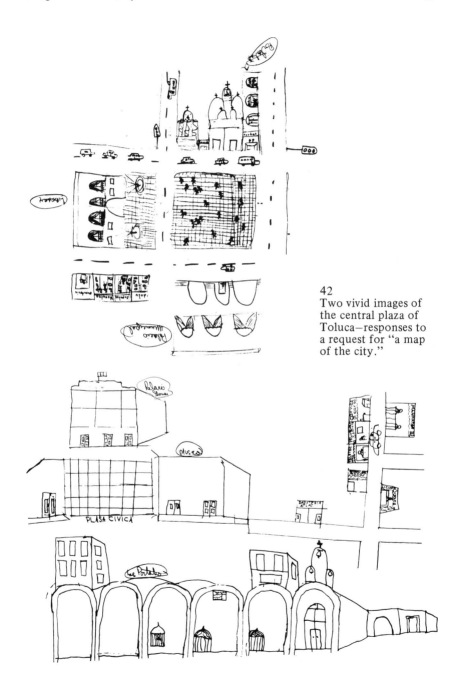

42
Two vivid images of
the central plaza of
Toluca—responses to
a request for "a map
of the city."

shacks, the streets are unpaved, the open lots are littered with trash. This regular layout is surrounded
by dusty open fields, without vegetation of any kind.

Almost all the representations show Avenida
Lourdes, the main east-west street and its stores, and
usually depict the other east-west channels, while the
numerous cross streets are rarely identified. The area
covered ranges from one to as many as forty blocks.
The school is a key feature in the community; many
maps show details of its classrooms, play area, and
front gate.

The images of San Agustin show an interesting
dichotomy. One group (mostly boys) represent the
environment as a map of streets and blocks. Their
drawings are schematic and lack sensuous detail. They
include a key to the location of activities and serve as
a down to earth image of a highly repetitive environment. The other group (mostly girls) make pictorial
representations showing shops, parks, and green areas.
Their drawings are full of details embellished with
textures, ornaments, and splashes of color. These
sensuous representations seem almost as if they were
an escape from a harsh environment—an escape accomplished by the addition of color, trees where
none exist, or sloping house roofs where all are flat.

The reactions of the young boys and girls on the
west side of Melbourne are again dissimilar. Their
maps vary widely in extent, from the surroundings of
a single house to a region of six square kilometers.
Every map is essentially a street map. The streets are
drawn large; other locations are appended as small
rectangles along them. Each child shows his own
house, and most show the houses of their friends. The
great majority indicate various shopping areas; a few
main roads, such as Churchill and Ballarat, also appear frequently. Other main roads are shown only on
a scattering of maps, since these map areas simply
overlap and do not coincide. The maps include various

schools, one particular park, and a football oval. Bus stops are rather frequently indicated. No consistent section of the river is mentioned, nor is any particular one of the widely distributed public reserves. Several children draw their high school, but as many depict factories, a pedestrian overpass, and a paddock for horses. Most of the children would probably be able to direct you to those things if asked, but they do not come spontaneously to mind when they are mapping their home grounds. They have difficulties in recording the neatly planned, basically rectangular, but frequently interrupted, layout of the streets. There is evidence that they know a much larger area in the western suburbs than they choose to show, since when challenged they readily enlarge their drawings. They are very conscious of the mosaic of separate suburban governments that surrounds them.

Their image of the central city is much poorer. It is usually a conventional, but imperfectly known, street grid, thinly set with some commercial locations, which are often misplaced. A single meandering route connects this grid with their own area, like a long umbilical cord. One has the impression that many of these boys and girls know a broad western region as well as the way to the city center, but that they know little of the center itself, and less of the remainder of Melbourne. Unfortunately, they may have understood (since the word "city" commonly refers to the center city only) that a map of the central business district was wanted rather than a map of the entire urban region. Thus, these drawings are inconclusive. At any rate, they have no vivid image of that central district, while the Salta and Cracow children display a clear conception of their downtown plaza with its historic buildings.

The Melbourne home region has no definite boundaries, no center. In the direct, physical sense, it cannot be viewed from above, as Salta can be, nor can it be

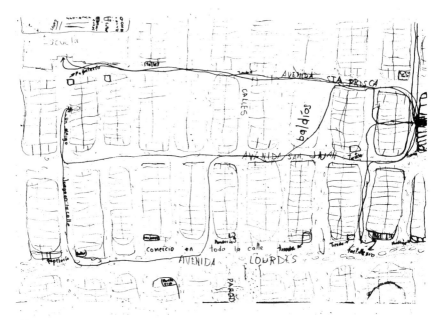

43
Two maps of San
Augustin: one a
practical guide; the
other, a wishful
image of home and
its appendages.

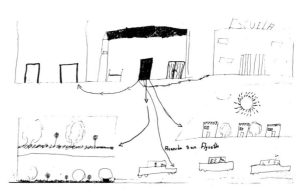

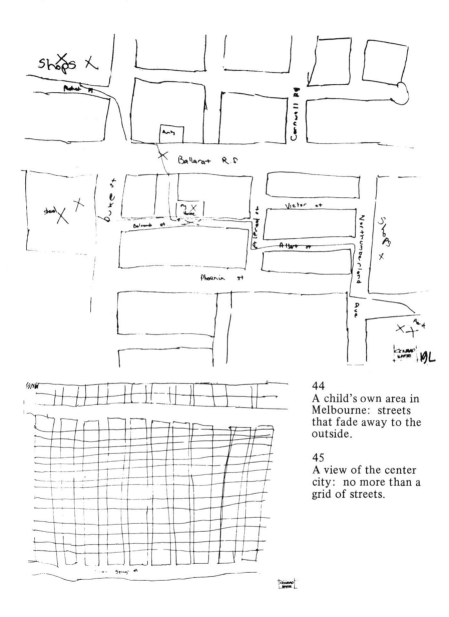

44
A child's own area in
Melbourne: streets
that fade away to the
outside.

45
A view of the center
city: no more than a
grid of streets.

seen as being within its bounds, as Bystra can. The
social facilities are the conventional sports fields and
schools. The playgrounds are featureless and empty.
The asphalted, treeless streets are equally empty. The
houses seem solid and comfortable, but the yards appear unused, except for sheds. (The Las Rosas yards
are full of house extensions—chicken yards, work
areas, and vine-covered dining places. The Bystra
yards are the working areas of the farms. Kozłowka
has only the trampled public spaces between its
buildings. There are a few small private gardens in
Zatrasie, which are fiercely defended against the children.) Wasteland in Melbourne is difficult to reach,
and rules prevent children from digging, building, or
bike riding on public land. The community is pleased
about an improvement to Dobson's Reserve and the
hope of a swimming pool, but they wait for an outside authority to accomplish it for them. (The Las
Rosas people are building their own pool on a hill
that no one controls.)

The Australian scene is almost perfectly unmanip-
ulable by its children, except that they can move
through it. In the air photos, one can see the tracks of
their movement. They walk the streets with their
friends. They hope to be some place else in the future. Their negative feelings are reinforced by the
newspapers, which assure them that they are at the
bottom and that they have no initiative. These feelings contrast strangely with the physical appearance
of the adolescents in the photographs—tall, well
dressed, almost mature, apparently full of vitality.

Favorite Places

When asked where they like best to be, where they
feel most at ease, where it is best to meet friends and
to be alone, the Melbourne children answer consistently: their own room, at home, or even better, at

the homes of friends. The responses of the children of Salta are the same, but they also add: the plaza, the local street corners, and some, the hills. The Polish children reply: at home, in the parks and woods, the streets, the homes of friends. Those from Toluca say much the same, although they emphasize playgrounds rather than streets. If asked where they least like to be, children will say school, boring places, where they are under control or have no friends. A few will mention places they believe to be dangerous, and several Australians and Poles say that home is where they least like to be. For those Ecatepec children who suggested such places, the answers were consistent: vacant lots with dirt and rocks, open areas full of trash, busy, narrow streets. In sharp contrast, they consistently named their school as a favorite place and gave it a loving emphasis on their maps. We can only suspect that for them the school is a welcome relief from the harsh reality of poverty that surrounds them—an oasis of stimulating experience where the children can do new things and read books that open up the wonders of the world. This must be a tribute to the public education in Ecatepec, and points to the important role that schools can play in the lives of poor children.

When they were asked to describe the best place imaginable to live in, their utopias also reflected consistent themes: trees, friends, quiet, lack of traffic, small size, cleanliness. (The repeated emphasis in Salta on kindness and a united people may indeed reflect some hidden anxieties.) It is remarkable how differences tend to level out in describing this ideal. Many children in all four nations describe rural scenes or rural villages, while others advocate center-city excitements. The Saltese, Tolucans, and Bystrans most often picture a village or an improved residential area much like their own, while the center-city Poles frequently describe a city with futuristic

"If I'm alone, then I like to be in the woods. I walk and think there." *Bystra*

"I feel free when I'm alone, when I am walking in the mountains by myself, simply if I'm all alone or swimming across a lake." *Kozłowka*

"Also, I like to travel by train. . . . To Huehetoca, it's a pueblo . . . about ten hours by train. . . . It's very pretty. I like it because there are trees, there's country, there are horses to ride. . . ." *Ecatepec*

"Bystra is the best place to live in. It's very pleasant when there are lots of woods near, and it's very green. There is pure air, and the cars don't roar past." *Bystra*

"In the countryside in a small house with trees surrounding it, a garden with roses, a brook, near some hills, with horses, but not to live alone." *Las Rosas*

"A place like this one." *Las Rosas*

"If she has her choice later on it'd be better not to live here." *Melbourne*

46
Rural peace: the environmental ideal of a Kleparski child.

47
Another Kleparski child has different hopes for the future.

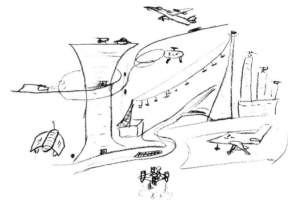

48
A Kozłowka child wishes for a modern house in a dramatic natural setting.

overtones. But those in the peripheral housing projects nominate one of the other situations as the ideal. The Melbournites talk of Europe, or of cities and seasides far away. The Ecatepecs speak of living on the ocean, or in the United States in southern California.

The Melbourne girls and boys want to be more independent of their parents, to range even more widely. Those of Salta are conscious of few barriers to their present movements, although they actually use their freedom less than one might think. The restrictions that the Argentine and Mexican children are most conscious of pertain to those places that arouse their curiosity, but before which parents and other adults have set barriers: the adult movies, certain clubs and bars. In the same fashion, the Polish children also say they are generally free to do what they wish. (Although an outsider's impression, judging from superficial observations of street behavior, the use of locks on apartment elevators, and similar clues, is that they are actually under close and constant adult control). All speak of the dangers that surround them: natural dangers (as in the rivers and forests), but above all the hazards of traffic and of the threatened assaults of "bad people," "hoods," "hooligans," or drunks.

Beautiful and Ugly Places

Beautiful places for the Australians include all the gardens, parks, and trees to be found somewhere else. Ugliness is a compound of their own factories, "old" houses, impersonal public buildings, pollution and rubbish. For a few of them, it seems to be ugly everywhere in the world. For most of the Ecatepecs, too, there were no beautiful places in their colonia, although some mentioned what little "green" areas there were: a small garden in front of the market, an arboleda. Some could not name beautiful places

"I try not to go out in the evenings, because it's unpleasant in the back lanes. Sometimes I'm scared out of my wits. In the evenings the hooligans are about, they might even set a dog on you. I run away." *Kozłowka*

"The bar is the worst here. The drunks sing and shout. I'm afraid to pass it." *Bystra*

"It isn't a place, it's the whole of Kozłowka that is dangerous, because the ruffians rove around, and it's very unpleasant to meet them in the dark. And in Cracow the streets, the crossings, are dangerous. The traffic is awful." *Kozłowka*

"It's dangerous deep in the woods because there may be mad animals. But here in the village it isn't." *Bystra*

"You can't be safe anywhere, really! People jump out at you in the dark!" *Melbourne*

"There is nothing beautiful here. Koz-łowka is quite nice, but you can't say it is beautiful." *Kozłowka*

"All around is ugly— it's a slum. The houses aren't looked after; people haven't got much money." *Melbourne*

"The plaza [is beautiful] because it is a happy place and there are always children playing."

"The hill in springtime is like a green pillow." *Las Rosas*

"The spring in the woods is holy. If somebody has no appetite and drinks water from it then his appetite will come back." *Bystra*

anywhere. The Tolucan children, on the other hand, named a great number of beautiful places; although they disagreed as to just which places were beautiful except that most nominated a city park on a small hill that is distinctly visible in the flat cityscape. The Argentines likewise named long lists of places they think beautiful, from their own plaza, their "flowery" local streets and deforested hills, to the plazas, parks, and monuments of the center city. Taken for a walk in the center, the children felt that the principal dimensions of beauty were cleanliness and modernity. They liked new stores, luminous signs, and multistory apartments. The Australians, with their broader city experience, disliked their apartment buildings but agreed about cleanliness. When the Polish village children drew pictures of the worst environment they could imagine, they showed shabby, traditional rural houses, heaps of litter, broken equipment, unsanitary conditions, and places selling alcohol. Most Salta children said there were no ugly places, but a few admitted the prison and certain city streets outside their own community to this class. The prison hides something fearful, but its battlemented walls are also romantic. This mixture of fear and romance parallels their ambivalent feelings for the hills.

We asked them to name any holy places, but sacredness is not an inherent feature of the landscape for most of these children. The only exceptions were two of the Polish villagers who named a woodland spring and an ancient tree, and two from Cracow who cited historic buildings (and another who nominated a police station since one couldn't use swear words there!). To most children, a holy place is simply a church, although some Australians and Poles say there are no holy places, and the Mexicans do not even mention the churches. But perhaps our question was wrong, if we wished to uncover any feelings of awe. For example, while the Tolucan children will not designate any part of their landscape as sacred, yet their city is the provincial capital and they consistently name the "palacias" of the administration, judiciary, and legislature, all set around the central plaza, as first on the list of important places. One senses here a certain respect and pride, at least, if not awe. Some Polish children have similar feelings about the historic monuments of Cracow.

Change

The children of Salta think there have been minor physical changes in their area, all for the better. They believe that the next ten years will see continued improvement. The Bystrans have seen rapid changes in the last years, social and economic as well as physical, and are eager for more. Most Tolucan children remember changes: new schools and playgrounds, paved streets, sidewalks, telephone lines, lights, water, drainage. Others mentioned more houses, more people, more stores. Most thought these changes were for the better and had no regrets. The Ecatepec children remember similar changes and are pleased: there is less dust now, houses that used to be shanties are fully constructed, one does not have to go outside the colonia for certain services. One child did think there were too many people, another regretted the building up of the vacant lots where children used to wander around. The Australians have seen changes too, but are less certain of their value. Some past changes have progressively restricted their freedom of action. They envision pervasive change in the future: new people, new ethnic groups, more apartments, more noise, pollution, crowding, and traffic. They are quite divided as to whether the future will be better or worse, although they are sure they don't like apartments and traffic. The children of central Cracow and Warszawa are less conscious of the future, but do

"The place where I live has changed for the better. New brick houses have been built. The wooden bridges have been changed for concrete ones. People work in factories now, but before they only worked on farms. . . . Living is more comfortable, and people earn more. More could be changed if all the people could be encouraged to work together." *Bystra*

"Always everything better, more developed." *Las Rosas*

"It's much cleaner with paving because before there was dust and one had to clean daily, daily. And when it rained, it was muddy, and very ugly." *Ecatepec*

"It will be all flats
and units with no
back yards for the
kids to play in."

"I don't think it will
change. . . . There'll
be different national-
ities around, more
road accidents . . .
more crowding."
Melbourne

have some forebodings—especially about traffic. Those
from Zatrasie and Kozłowka have perhaps experienced the greatest rush of construction. Like the
Australians, they are unsure of how well they like it.
Only three children of Salta think they will leave
their area in the future; only three children of Melbourne think they will remain.

All the children would like to see more trees, better streets, and more recreation facilities. The Argentines want more tall buildings, supermarkets, and
bars, while the Australians want to tear down the
factories and stop the growth of apartment flats. The
center-city children in Poland want more places to
play in, while their comrades on the periphery want
more activities and services and better access to the
center. The Tolucan children want more parks and
playgrounds, a cleaner and more beautiful environment, control of traffic, lower taxes and prices, an
abolition of bars, factories, and even the military
base. All these groups believe they have little power
to affect the environment, although one Melbourne
boy helps to maintain a small park, the villagers join
in keeping their houses and yards, and several Salta
children speak of working in the hills, improving the
school, or participating in the Christmas pageant.

The children of Ecatepec think of the whole
colonia and its people. They want more and better
schools—including vocational schools where they can
learn skills—more parks and playgrounds. They want
better provision of basic necessities: drinking water,
clinics, housing, transportation. One spoke of free land
for the poor, another wanted to help poor children go
to school, another looked for ways of giving money
to parents. Their suggestions reflect a genuine concern
for their families, as well as their own future, and an
empathy for fellow residents of the colonia. They
search for ways out of poverty and indignity and look
to their schools for more education, more skill.

These adolescents are aware of the pervasive changes around them, but they perceive those changes with different feelings and with a different degree of accuracy. They sense their own growth. The exterior changes are landmarks along their own internal path of development. There are constant hints as to how their knowledge and use of the city (and the restrictions that city and adults put on them) continue to change as they grow. They learn and they teach one another within this changing relationship. In a few years, they will use and value their environment in quite a different way. The Salta report, for example, hints at the destructive power of the older adolescents, of their idleness and boredom, and their attacks upon the school.

"It would be nice to make the school higher, and fence it in or close it off with railings, because the boys that have nothing to do break what is inside." *Las Rosas*

Parents and Officials

The interviews with parents and officials (not carried out in Mexico and Poland) are perhaps less revealing, but they corroborate much of what the children say. At this age, parents are still in control and fairly well informed of what their children are doing. Their own hard-working childhoods, rural or urban, contrast with the improved position of their offspring in terms of material goods. They see the future much as their children do. While the standard of living rises, the children have followed (and in the future expect and are expected to follow) much the same path their parents traversed. The times are better, but the quality of personal life has not changed that rapidly. In Melbourne, at least, even the environment seems no better.

"I think she'll have a clean, homely and happy house and be just like her mother—bored, overworked, and housebound." *Melbourne*

The officials are, for the most part, well ignorant of what the children do. Despite the lack of use of the existing facilities, the Australian planners think that space for organized team sport is needed most. The Zatrasie district is considered a model of planned development. The official interviews were few and scattered, but two trends were apparent. First, the childhood places of these officials were strikingly different from those of the children under study. Second, whatever substantive knowledge may or may not be gained by these last interviews, it is evident that they are an excellent way of informally communicating research findings and for locating a chink from which to dislodge some fragments from the smooth face of official policy.

Policy Implications: Environmental Improvement

These studies have numerous policy indications, at least for these children in these localities, and perhaps more generally. In light of their importance for social interaction and informal play, the form and regulation of local streets and small open spaces is one critical issue. Traffic hazards can be reduced by installing lights, or bumps, and by periodic, or permanent, street closings. Layouts that deter through-traffic can be avoided. Dead-end streets have always been excellent places for play. Traffic can be diminished or diverted by more general policies as well. Sidewalks can be widened in places, or integrated with small play spaces, even with sharply limited resources. Underused or abandoned rights of way, wastelands, and other "left-over" spaces can be made safe and utilized for children's recreation. Such areas would serve as a necessary supplement to the traditional parks and playgrounds, which do not allow for creative play. The littered Maribyrnong River, shut off by factories and a golf course, is an unexploited resource in Melbourne. So are the scattered lots and the bridge approaches in crowded Powisle. So too is the sterile lake bed around the colonia in Ecatepec.

The hunger for trees is outspoken and seemingly universal. Landscaping should be as essential a part of the basic infrastructure of a settlement as electricity, water, sewers, and paving. It is not window dressing. In a hostile environment like Ecatepec, soil improvement, or even soil importation, must be a priority in providing open space. Moreover, unlike extending utilities or paving, children can join in landscaping their neighborhood.

Community Identity

The children should be living in places that have a clear social and spatial identity, places they can understand and take pride in. They should have a role to play in community maintenance and community celebration—particular functions to perform, particular places for which they are at least in part responsible. Their sense of past and future should be connected to their locality, related to the conservation of natural resources and to their historical heritage. The locality itself should have features that make it amenable to changes that children can accomplish. The improvements made to the small, resident-owned houses of Bystra and Las Rosas exemplify how environments can have a form that facilitates user control. Centrally managed streets, playgrounds, and apartment yards can easily become dispiriting. The children of Melbourne and Poland may be right in their opposition to the new flat buildings. Waste grounds offer another potential for this type of local action—the Las Rosas pool is one example.

Institutional Advocacy and Responsive Planning

Planners, designers, and environmental managers will have to become more concerned with children's needs. Observation and research should be part of the design process. The child client, if accessible, should be asked to evaluate the existing environment and to participate in the design and construction of settings specifically intended for children. But it is clear, if children's rights and needs are to be represented in public decisions, that there must be formal bodies concerned with children's welfare at the local and national levels. Many countries have such institutions; UNESCO has its own commission. Without such formal institutions, this or similar studies will have very little impact.

Access and Education

The city should open out to these children. They want both quiet and stimulus and should find both close at hand. The relation of residential areas and city services is not only important for adult welfare but for the child's welfare as well. It may be more critical for the latter, since the child is more limited in his range and has the greater hunger for stimulus because his growth feeds on it. Attractive public places, where interesting activity can be seen and engaged in, should be accessible to children. Once a settlement is located, access may be created by new bus routes or schedules, by the elimination or reduction of fares for children, or by weekend bus service to attractive places. Hours of opening and closing may be shifted to accommodate child users. There are real problems of heavy traffic and personal assault to cope with. Children may be taught to move about the city. With greater confidence, and fewer official or transport restrictions, they might learn to use the diverse city as a learning ground. Experiencing a spectrum of places, people, and activity will reduce their boredom (even their vandalism?), and deepen their development, which comes to the same thing.

The schools themselves would be more interesting if they used the local environment in their teaching. Most activities for these children are highly programmed. They spend much of the day in the classroom and have little time to explore the city. Schools might emphasize experiential learning more frequently, using the city and region as an educative resource. The case of Ecatepec points out the potential of the school as an oasis and a hope.

Television is rapidly becoming a major way in which children throughout the world experience reality. For poor children with limited mobility, it may be the only way they can be exposed to the range of opportunities in a society. While essentially a passive medium, it can also be used for local environmental exploration and can be linked to school programs. Broadcasting agencies must become aware of the terrifying responsibility their programs bear.

Admittedly, these studies are too small to be useful as a firm basis for decision, much less as a source of generalized theory. We only intend to show that policy implications *can* be drawn from them.

Revisions of Method

From these first experiences, we draw a number of conclusions about better ways of conducting such studies. In doing so, we must keep in mind the aim: flexible research which can be done with modest means in almost any situation. Rather than elaborating the study, we should aim to abbreviate it while still permitting local elaboration according to interest. Unfortunately, some additions do seem to be inescapable.

The nature of the studies appears to have been chosen correctly. The work is rightly carried out and controlled by local research teams rather than by imported experts. However, a closer contact with the scientific advisor would be useful to the local teams. A personal visit by the advisor to each locality and a detailed discussion with the local team is highly recommended for future research.

The environment is critical for this age; low income groups are those most affected by it; the immediate locality is the crucial place. Beyond this, however, it may be wise to relax our original selection criteria, allowing local teams to pick subjects that fit directly into current policy issues—places where issues of environmental quality are critical and can be influenced. Since the link of research to policy is our prime concern, each investigation should promise information that will change some forthcoming decision. This determination can only be made on the ground. What we would hold to is that the study should deal with the way children use and value their settings and that it be made via open-ended dialog and observation, dealing in depth with a small number of children in a restricted locality, and if possible, producing some experimental evidence concerning the relevant perceptual clues.

We see several ways in which these studies might develop, given a relaxation of the selection criteria. In many nations, it might be more relevant to study children in the rural settlements, probing such things as their attitudes toward nature and the maintenance of landscape and culture, looking for hints on how they might later be induced to remain in the countryside rather than inundate the city, or conversely, on how they might be better prepared for urban life.

We would also like to know more about children in different stages of development—at six or nine years of age, for example, when they are using the spatial world most intensively, or in later adolescence when parental control is shed and alienation and destructiveness appear more openly. Indeed, where resources permit, longitudinal studies of children as they develop in their landscape would be ideal.

It now seems clear that an international comparison of childhood attitudes may be much less important

than comparative studies in the same culture and region, such as those carried out in Mexico and Poland.
Studies would compare microlocations differing from
each other in specific traits of environment, age, or
class. Building a regional patchwork of modest sample
studies would be the most efficient way of informing
decisions and of building local research capability. We
advocate an extension of the range of the sampling
rather than an extension of the size of the areas
studied, the size of the sample population, or the
multiplicity of research techniques to be employed.
The sampling should be a modest, continuing effort
directed to clarifying local problems; yet it should be
sufficiently coordinated so as to allow a flow of information between national teams as well as the
publication of comparative results when something
interesting turns up.

Describing the Environment Itself

The research techniques can be clarified and simplified to some degree. The photographic grid proved to
be an excellent and relatively undemanding way of
describing the spatial setting. Where it was not used
systematically, we feel the lack of a fundamental description, both of the environment and of the visible
behavior. The recommended scale of the grid had to
be modified in the extensive Melbourne region, but
proved about right in Las Rosas, although some additional shots were required. Two improvements can be
suggested. First, it is important to photograph the
nearest accessible outdoor space to the grid point if
we are to get a reasonable systematic description.
Both photographic collections are almost entirely
confined to the public streets. Back yards, factory
premises, and other such spaces are rarely shown, or
appear only incidentally from a distance. These latter
places, however, are typical features of the setting,

49
A fragment from the
photogrid of Mel-
bourne: how photo-
graphs taken at
regular intervals cap-
ture the look of an
entire setting.

even when they are inaccessible to the children. Of course, they may also be inaccessible to the photographer, but some reasonable effort should be made to record them. The aerial photographs look down into these pieces of terrain, but they are much more useful if a few sample ground shots can be correlated with the aerial view.

Second, having arrived at a grid intersection, the photographer needs better instructions as to where to point his camera, unless we ask him to make a 360-degree panorama, which would surely be expensive and redundant. He can be asked to look for evidence of children's activity, for barriers to access, for ways in which the setting has been modified by its users, for visible pollution, for levels of maintenance, or for whatever is expected to be critical in the study. A checklist of this kind, coupled with standard instructions about lenses and sky exposure, would produce a more relevant and more consistent survey. (See the Melbourne report for a discussion of some of these points.)

The aerial photographs are extremely useful. Together with the ground photographs, they produce much relevant information. They would be even more informative if stereo-pairs were provided, and if they were correlated with ground views in every typical situation, since the landscape could then be read in detail.

Given these two kinds of photographs, the required maps can be simpler than originally specified. They need only be outline affairs, which key the locations of the photos, illustrate the relation of the children's community to the city as a whole and to points of interest to the children, and which name the environmental features or describe particular land uses. Given a good photographic base, the maps can therefore be quickly and freely executed, or investigators can make use of standard maps already available.

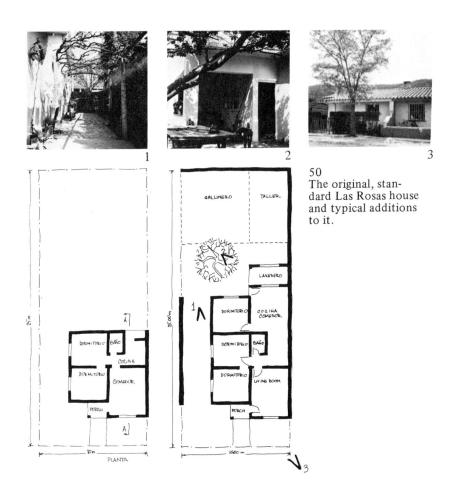

50
The original, stan-
dard Las Rosas house
and typical additions
to it.

Inside the Home

It has become quite apparent, however, that in one respect these studies must be extended. Since so much time is spent indoors, it is necessary to get some record of the typical house interior. The Salta study included useful plans of original and remodeled houses and yards in Las Rosas. A casual remark in the course of reporting the parent's interview indicates that the furnishing and use of these rooms may be critical in the children's lives. The degree of crowding in the home seemed to be a significant factor in the actions and attitudes of the Polish children as well. In the future, studies should include a few sketch house and yard plans, showing furnishings, density of occupation, and activity areas. If possible, these sketches should be accompanied by photographs of house interiors. Such descriptions will mean a substantial increase in the research load. Moreover, it may be difficult to gain access to the houses or to have the opportunity to make plans on the spot. Successful interior photography is more difficult, both technically and socially, than snapshots taken in the street. Nevertheless, the gain seems worth the effort. The interior-exterior contrasts, the lengthy time spent before the television set, the importance of a child's own room and furniture, all indicate that a focus on outdoor space alone is inadequate.

House plans need not be precisely to scale and can be drafted freehand by someone accustomed to such work. Moreover, only those parts of the house most relevant to the child—his own room, the dining area, the television space—need be recorded in detail. Since future interviews will also deal with interior space, the portions of the house to be recorded will be indicated by how the interview data indicates what the child is preoccupied with.

However, any field recording of the house interior may be regarded as an intrusion on family privacy and in that case it must be omitted. Descriptions will then be reduced to rough sketches and word pictures made after a house visit. Just as in making exterior descriptions, attention in the house interior should be paid to such things as evidence of use, of territory, and of user modification. In the same vein, the children may be asked to sketch their own image of their dwelling and its territories. What we seek is the comprehensive description of indoors and outdoors as a used landscape—an ecology of children.

See Florence Ladd, "Black Youths View Their Environments."

Observing Behavior

While the naturalistic observation of child behavior outdoors was quite successful, judging from the one example we have, it was sadly missed in the other cases. The diagrams, supplemented by photographs and notes were a useful innovation in recording such behavior. But the diagrams were deficient in recording movement—the constant shifting of groups and their activities. The technique will have to be modified to record dynamic aspects of this kind, since making an entire series of "instantaneous" records would be staggering to compile and staggering to read.

Deficient in this one respect, the diagrams turn out to be unnecessarily elaborate in others. Since photographs were taken to show the activity being diagrammed (and this should clearly always be done), many of the physical details, so carefully recorded in the diagram, are also in clear view on the photograph; other such details may be irrelevant to the action. The diagram, once it is made capable of showing change, can then be reduced to a record of action with only as much of the setting as is relevant to that action, or is not visible in the photograph, or is needed to give the spatial context of that photograph. This will simplify the drafting as well as the reading of the diagrams. The photographs capture dress and gross behavior. The observer should note the motion, the fine behavior, and speech where possible, and should emphasize how children actively use the spatial features around them. Some of this escaped our recordings.

Not only should diagrams be accompanied by one or more photographs, but it might also be useful to videotape some sequences of child activity. Both the Salta and the Melbourne studies produced movies illustrating the chosen setting. These are attractive records, useful for presentation to an audience. But they really come alive whenever they happen to show the children in action. Movies and videotapes are ideally suited to record activity. Otherwise, the other records describe the static, physical place better, and by simpler means. In any case, it is essential to note the actual behavior of the children, as well as what they say about it. Both investigations illuminate each other.

As a last comment on the field recording, we would ask for a better picture of the historical development of the chosen place. Historic maps, or photographs of its condition prior to its building or its occupation by the present generation, are valuable records. The way an environment has changed and is changing, what that change means, and to what extent the children are aware of it are central issues. Any landscape is always a landscape in change. Unfortunately, very little historical data was developed in the studies at hand, although the previous condition of the landscape can often be inferred from other material.

The Individual Interviews

As predicted, the interviews with the children were rather long, but they produced a great deal of

CANBERRA
BATHURST

A5

51
Diagramming the
activity in a public
park in Melbourne
and a photograph
keyed to the diagram.

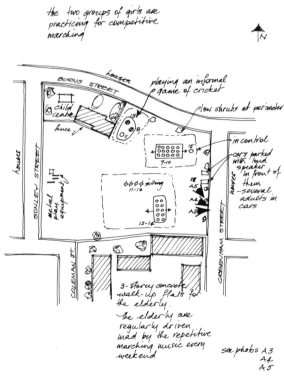

the two groups of girls are
practicing for competitive
marching

playing an informal
game of cricket

low shrubs at perimeter

in control

cars parked
with loud
speaker
in front of
them
—several
adults in
cars

3-storey concrete
walk-up flats for
the elderly

the elderly are
regularly driven
mad by the repetitive
marching music every
weekend

se photos A3
          A4
          A5

SPATIAL OBSERVATION FIELD NOTATION
KEY

● male   ○ female

● ○ child.   on bicycle.

▲ △ adult.

$●^{14}$ male child of 14 years.

⬭ vehicle.

← direction of movement.

←——— ← path of travel

φ passive at time of observation.

○—○ communicating.

[●○] co-operating.

(○ ○) approximation of behavioural
      territory.

► A37 indicates position of descriptive
      photo showing activity
      with reference number.

Other notation symbols available
but not used in present observations:

∝ interacting with, using, or modifying
                  environment.

●⟩ constrained or frustrated by environment.

●⟩●⟨ in conflict with each other.

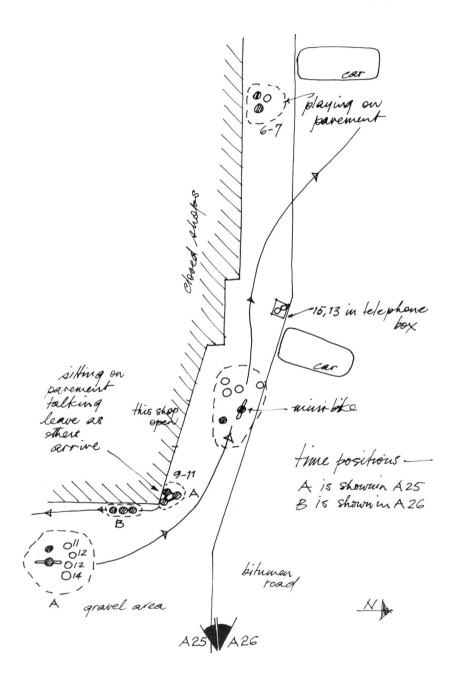

car

playing on pavement

6-7

closed shops

15,13 in telephone box

car

sitting on pavement talking leave as others arrive

this shop open

mini-bike

time positions
A is shown in A25
B is shown in A26

9-11

A

B

11
12
12
14

A   gravel area

bitumen road

N

A25   A26

52
It is much harder to
catch the action when
it is flowing along the
streets.

A26

interesting material. It takes a period of time to gain the confidence of the children, but the interviews themselves can be conducted within a reasonable block of time (two weeks in Salta, but the part-time interviews in Melbourne spread out over two months). While a few deletions in the questions can be suggested, a larger number of intriguing additions must be made. Because of this, and to prevent an otherwise inevitable bloating, the interview should be reorganized into two parts: a brief "core" recommended for all occasions, plus a longer list of possible additions designed to obtain special information. The use of the latter would depend on local interest.

These modifications may be compared to the original questions listed on pages 99-101.

We recommend that the following items be retained in the "core" after the preliminaries of questions 1 and 2 (identification and residential history):

1. the mapping of their area and of their use of it (question 4 in the original guidelines);
2. a verbal description of their area (original question 5, but substantially modified);
3. dangers and frustrations (part of original questions 10 and 12);
4. territory and control (part of original question 11);
5. preferences (part of original question 10);
6. what changes have occurred, whether they are for the better, and views on the future (part of original questions 14 and 15); and
7. a day in detail (original question 18).

These are the questions that have produced the most useful information; they also seem most universal in their application.

The "own area" maps, for example, are full of information on what the children consider important, how they put it together, the range of their knowledge, their feelings, activities, and confusions. Although studies elsewhere have reported difficulty in persuading some people to draw such maps and have cast doubts on their value as a reflection of the mental image, the results with these children contradict this impression. As a nonverbal technique, like photographs and videotape, they cut through language difficulties and reveal feelings and concepts that otherwise do not surface. Placement, sequence, scale, and style all say something and are permanently recorded, in contrast to most questionnaire interviews where intonation and expression tend to be lost. Undoubtedly, mapping is an obstacle in some adult interviews, but the children, at least in mapping their local area, attacked it with conviction. While it should only be one part of an analysis, the Polish team showed how much information could be extracted from only one aspect of these drawings. Moreover, much can be seen in these drawings, even from a great geographical and cultural distance.

In the future, the sketches should be more carefully keyed to "true" maps of objective locations in the area. This could be accomplished by indicating the overlapping boundaries of the areas drawn, transposed to true scale on an accurate map, and also by asking the investigator to name the obscure points on the drawings or to sketch the true pattern as an appended diagram (as was done occasionally in Melbourne). Simple counts of the elements shown are also useful. The request itself (old question 4) can be simplified, since the most productive sources are, first, the map of "the area you live in" (how they choose to understand that phrase is in itself revealing), and second, the additions (preferably in another color) that show what parts of the area they actively use or frequent. But asking the children to redraw a map (because it seems thin or restricted or incorrect) simply distorts the information.

The first part of question 10 on the obstacles to action must also be reformulated, in a more concrete way, to get at the specific difficulties children encounter in using the physical, spatial environment. In addition, the question should be broken into two parts. The other core questions seemed workable, except that question 18 (yesterday's events in detail) must be more rigorously applied and recorded so that a time budget can be constructed from it with confidence. A detailed diary of activity on a specific day that is fresh in the memory is wanted rather than a general estimate of how much time is spent doing this or that. The data should be recorded on a form divided into half-hour time periods, showing the location and nature of activity. (See the Melbourne report for an excellent example.) All the questions need rewording so that they naturally refer to interior space, as well as to the outdoors.

Some of the remaining questions can be recommended as additions, but modifications are also indicated in this group. Question 3 (on daily actions) is unnecessary if question 18 is completed. Questions 6 and 7 (on the knowledge and use of other areas) were useful but not central; they could be combined. Question 9 (on freedom of movement) can be added to this group, and also reduced, since it has redundancies in it. Question 8 (map of the whole city) is usefully related to the local map in question 4; however, it must be emphasized that an idea of the *entire* city or urban region, not just its central core, is wanted. Some children have substantial trouble with making a city map, which is of course in itself revealing. Question 11 (on being at home) is ambiguous, since "at home," "at ease," and "able to do what you want," can all be different things. The most interesting part of this question pertained to belonging and control, which was made into a core question. Question 13 (beautiful and holy places) is sometimes an evocative question, but not always. "Holy" is often very narrowly understood. Question 16 (the best place to live in) is useful (as is its inverse, "describe the worst environment"), but less so than the description of what the children are actually experiencing. It has shown some interesting consistencies, but the replies are rarely very imaginative. In using question 17 (happiest and saddest days), the local teams usually deleted the "saddest day" question as potentially disturbing. And if the "happiest day" is asked for, it must be reformulated to refer to concrete qualities in the environment.

Other questions can be added to this elective list. In addition to being asked to map their neighborhood, the children could be asked to map their own room, house, and yard, and to describe what they do in each place. Useful discussions can be developed around representative photographs of places in their area, as well as typical locales elsewhere in the city, if such photos are taken prior to the interview. The children would be asked to identify the views, to describe what they do in each area, what the place means to them, what they like or dislike about it, and so forth. This is a tested and evocative technique. Children could make models, instead of maps, of their area, and could act out a day's activity in those models.

Special feelings can be investigated. For example, the children might be asked more specifically about their attitudes toward nature, animals, and plants, and their use of them. As in the Tolucan study, the stresses they encounter because of pollution or climate might be probed. One could try to develop their sense of local environmental history, or to find out to what extent they learn from exposure to their environment, as contrasted with what they learn in school or through the media. Various standard psychological tests can be given, similar to those of the Polish team in regard to optimum levels of stimulus, in order to test the interaction of psychological and environmental variables. Projective methods are possible in which children are encouraged to tell stories about pictures that show other children acting in the environment—playing in a wild place, sitting on a stair, visiting a center city, helping to build a house, listening to a teacher in a schoolroom, riding a crowded bus—in other words, an image of young people as they might act in that culture, but which can be interpreted in different and revealing ways.

The child's use of the social network in his locality can also be probed, as in the simple and effective technique suggested by Dr. Ayala and employed by the Polish group. In choosing among all these possibilities, however, the research must neither be overloaded with technique nor should its focus on the spatial environment be lost to view. Moreover, great care must be taken not to impose the values of the interviewer, or to encourage the child to give expected, "adult" answers. This is by no means easy.

Group Exercises

In sum, the interview was basically correct and useful, but needs repair and should be reorganized into a brief common core with a longer list of elective procedures. We also urge that the studies include one or more group exercises, as outlined in the original guidelines. While the other teams were unable to carry this through, the Salta team conducted several group events with most interesting results. The discussions on top of the San Bernando Hill, and while walking along Caseros Street, produced many feelings and perceptions that would never have come out except in a relaxed and open discussion in the presence of the environment itself. In some ways, these talks are the most interesting parts of the Argentine relation.

Again, we can list a number of elective possibilities for this group work. The old guidelines talked of small conferences and also of city tours (which the

Salta team carried out). One can also think of asking the children to take an interviewer on a tour of their own area, to point out its features and their meaning on the spot. Films, photographs, and diagrams previously produced can be used as discussion material. Even better, if resources permit, the children may be asked to make drawings, photographs, or even films of features of the environment that interest them. Experiments in imagining and analyzing potential changes may also be made (again, as in Salta), but with due care that these experiments are not taken as promises for action that in fact will never happen. Moreover, these latter procedures require ample preparation in order to allow the children to understand their own interests and to break free of stereotyped solutions. When the Polish children were asked to suggest changes they would make "if they were the architects," they made plans very similar to those that architects normally make—plans not particularly congruent to their own experience and interests. Social roles are powerful, even in the imagination.

See Roger Hart, "The Child's Landscape in a New England Town," for some fascinating examples of tours conducted by children.

In some cases, it might be possible to carry these experiments forward into actual participation in local change or maintenance. Or, the work of the children may be directed toward making teaching material for other children engaged in similar studies, or for use in school. One can imagine a group movie, or an exhibition, for example, by which one set of children communicate their sense of their own places and lives to children in other areas. In other words, the studies can branch out in many ways, given imagination and an understanding of local need.

Planners and Parents

The interviews with parents and official planners may also be put on the elective list. In the two cases at hand, the interviews with parents produced less information than the interviews with children, although they did corroborate the former and also showed how often the children's ways of acting and believing followed parental patterns. They also had indirect advantages, such as legitimating the research in parental eyes and giving interviewers easy access to the houses. But in both cases parental interviews could have been dropped without loss of any essential information. In other situations, where parents may be badly misinformed about child activity, these interviews may be more important. In any case, they raise ethical issues about the danger of communicating child attitudes or actions to parents without the consent of the former.

The interviews with the planners proved more useful, both as indicators of ignorance or misperception, and as a way of finding out how environmental decisions are made. Moreover, they give a legitimate entry for connecting the research to policy and for communicating research results. We would like to keep some interview of this kind as a regular part of the procedure, but its nature would have to vary a great deal according to local issues and organization. We retain a recall of the official's own childhood. At times it might be important to talk to engineers, to planners, to teachers, to people from an educational ministry, to welfare workers, or to political leaders. The choice would depend on where the information would make a difference.

We come back, then, to requiring a basic environmental description, some field observations of child behavior, and a core interview with the children as the absolutely essential parts of the study; these may be followed by an official interview, which can take varied forms. In addition, there would be a set of elective procedures that might be added to all these essential elements, including participative exercises and an interview with the parents. Although all of

this may require a bulkier guideline, yet the work itself will be simpler and more flexible. A recommended revised guideline is detailed on pages 81-99,
and may be compared to the original instructions
immediately following.

Extension of the Research

Given these modifications, we recommend that these
studies be extended to a significant number of nations and that they be carried on as a continuing
series under UNESCO supervision. In each country a
local team would choose the places and procedures
best suited to developing its own research capabilities
and to meeting local problems. UNESCO would be
responsible for initiating studies and coordinating the
work, modifying and developing techniques, and
maintaining a flow of information between nations,
including the arrangement of conferences and the
publishing of occasional comparative findings. For
this purpose, UNESCO should retain a scientific advisor who should have the funds necessary to carry
out this work, and who would make occasional visits
to local teams in the field. UNESCO should also be
able to pay for certain special costs of the local teams,
such as travel, consultation, publication, or unusual
equipment.

Initiating new studies requires the stimulation of
local interest and the location of appropriate local
teams and situations. It means that the advisor must
adapt the research guide to the specific situation of
each country and ensure that the research will not
only have its own internal validity but also be useful
for the pressing policy decisions of the nation concerned. Coordination requires that the national projects be linked together and that they also be
connected to other international efforts, such as the
MAB program on the perception of the environment,

and UNESCO work in public participation in decision making and on the social consequences of environmental change.

The naturalistic, open-ended techniques of dialogue and observation, which involve the children directly and openly and use graphic languages as well as verbal ones, must be continuously improved and modified to fit each new culture. The national work must be monitored and the Secretariat in Paris kept informed. Local teams should be kept in communication, exchanging information on their own work and on other work in the field. Small, brief group conferences between the active research teams have been extremely useful for this in the past. Occasionally, team members might be asked to participate in larger international conferences. The production of papers by the local teams and the recurrent publication of comparative conclusions will provide new elements in the analysis of urban settlement and will have direct practical usefulness. Simple and modest as these studies are, we feel that they will prove crucial in managing the human environment of the future.

Kevin Lynch
July 1975

ORIGINAL AND REVISED GUIDELINES

Based on experience with the first four national studies, we recommend the following guidelines for any future studies of the spatial environment of children. Following these recommended guidelines, we append some sections of the original research guide used in directing the first studies, since some readers may want to correlate the national studies with these old guidelines. Much of the material is repeated from one guide to the other, and so we present only those portions of the older guide that referred directly to procedures of observation and interview. The newer guide, on the other hand, is complete. The original guide was written by Dr. Tridib Banerjee and Prof. Kevin Lynch. The later modifications were made by Prof. Lynch.

Revised Research Guide for an International Study on the Spatial Environment of Children

Scope and Purpose

These studies focus on the way in which children use, image, and value their spatial environment, particularly where that is changing rapidly due to planned or induced development. We emphasize the immediate micro-environment, particularly house interiors and the nearby outdoor space; and concentrate on lower income groups in regions of low resource and rapid change.

Our purpose is to help document some of the human costs and benefits of economic development by showing how the child's use and perception of the resulting micro-environment affects his life and his personal development. Children are the fundamental resource of any society. In doing so, we hope to suggest policies and programs for improving the child's spatial environment in the course of national economic growth, or for improving the way he uses or learns from that environment, as well as to evaluate the effectiveness of any related existing policies and standards, such as those for education, housing, open space, environmental protection, or for the design and maintenance of public space and facilities.

While pursuing this primary objective, we may in part achieve some other relevant, if secondary, goals:
1. to develop a simple set of indicators of environmental quality, which can be used to evaluate the existing environment, or plans for future development, or changes over time;
2. to learn whether the quality of the micro-environment is currently improving or deteriorating in the developing countries in regard to its impact on

those human beings who are probably most dependent on it, and to show
how the child's environment has shifted from that of the previous generation;

3. to contrast the child's actual use and image of space with the educational
   planner's idea of what the child experiences and how he learns, or with the
   economic and physical planner's awareness of what his plans create for
   children;
4. to see what latent support for environmental improvement may exist in the
   basic values of the culture in indigenous institutions, and in the perceptions
   of ordinary people; and
5. to show, by a small concrete example, how a long-range international program of research about environmental quality may stimulate local research,
   which in turn can affect local or national development decisions.

Due to the wide variations under which these studies will be conducted, and
their small size, it must be clear, however, that they can neither be statistically
representative nor rigorously comparative.

The following research guide outlines a small study for attaining these ends.
The study will be based on concrete, open-ended, naturalistic observation of
children acting in their own environment, and on direct communication with
them as voluntary informants. Thus, we hope to learn how the world seems to
them. Necessarily, questions and experiments must make sense in the particular
culture concerned; therefore, the local analyst, using his familiarity with that
culture, must not only translate and adjust the details of this research protocol
but be ready to make modifications of unworkable or fruitless procedures.
Above all, he must be able to follow unexpected leads as the evidence develops,
not only avoiding the suppression of contradictory evidence but keeping alert
to what these children and their setting are telling him.

For each country studied, there will be a local research team, which must be
intimately acquainted with the local culture and be able to establish an easy
rapport with the low-income children and their parents. Since there is little experience anywhere in analyzing the interaction between man and environment,
nor any developed discipline in this area, the local team must probably be an
interdisciplinary one, consisting, at least, of a sociologist, psychologist, or
anthropologist, supported by a planner, architect, or geographer trained in
analyzing the spatial environment. In addition, the team will usually require a
"contact"—a local social worker, teacher, or community leader—who will be
able to bring them into direct and friendly communication with the particular
group to be studied. It is advisable that at least one member of the team be a

woman, since teenage girls and their mothers will be interviewed, and much more reliable communication is likely if the interviewer is also female. Whatever formal specialties they represent, or research techniques they are familiar with, all these people must, first of all, have a sharp eye and a sympathetic ear. They will need some secretarial support for preparing reports and transcribing interviews and a means of making and reproducing maps and photographs. But otherwise, no special equipment or elaborate support will be needed. The local teams will carry out the actual research and write a report on it.

In addition to these local teams, there will be an international coordinator, working in consultation with the Department of Social Sciences of UNESCO, who will guide and coordinate the work, develop techniques, maintain the flow of information, and be responsible for comparative reports and conferences.

Choice of Areas and Subjects

Three decisions are required to initiate the study: (1) to choose the general type of setting; (2) to select the particular locality and social group to be studied; and (3) to select the subjects themselves.

Selection of General Subject and Setting
The locations of settlements of the poor vary quite widely from country to country. It is not unreasonable to expect that the children brought up in the favelas of Sao Paulo or the barriadas of Lima, for example, located on the periphery of the city, will have different levels of access, exposure, and conceptions of the rest of the city than the children growing up in the slums of Calcutta or Tokyo, which are distributed fairly randomly in the central urban areas. Local investigators should choose the pattern that is characteristic for their own country. Areas that have undergone, or are currently undergoing, rapid change would be a natural choice. But subjects and settings should be chosen to fit current policy issues in the region, i.e., be places where issues of environmental quality are critical and where that quality can be influenced. Normally, the most critical issues are to be found among the lower-income groups living in areas of rapid change, whether it be inner city slum, peripheral squatter settlement, the haunts of homeless sidewalk dwellers, new working class housing, rural village, or whatever. For any particular country, the local investigators will be the most competent group to decide the place and people to be investigated. Clearly, these decisions will require an understanding of the

spatial distribution of the poor and a familiarity with public policies that impinge upon the lives of their children.

Selection of a Particular Socio-Spatial Unit
Within the chosen general setting, one then looks for a smaller socio-spatial unit from which actual subjects can be drawn. Since this research is exploratory and holistic, the case study of a small, defined, population group is more appropriate than a sample survey of a whole population. In some situations, as in India or Japan, where small clusters of 200 to 300 slum dwellings are scattered over the city, one such cluster would, in itself, provide a socially and territorially defined setting for this analysis. Elsewhere, one should look for a specific locality that is a microcosm of the large community and contains at least enough people at the chosen socio-economic level to include thirty or more children in the specified age group. It will be preferable if the social group has been fairly stable in the locality, so that the children were born there, or have been living there since early childhood. It will be easier if the residents think of themselves as some sort of unit, with a common origin, caste, or class. It will be useful if the locality has some territorial identity, some commonly felt sense of place, as is usually associated with such physical features as barriers, changes in use or density, common facilities, etc. But all these dimensions—temporal stability, and social and territorial identity—may have to be sacrificed if it is necessary to study a group typical of the chosen general conditions, such as a transient central slum, recent in-migrants, or sidewalk dwellers. Due to these wide variations among the groups to be studied, these analyses cannot be strictly comparative between nations. Within one country, however, it is feasible and useful to make comparative analyses of children in different spatial settings, or of different age or class, or of more or less recent residence. Successive samples can gradually extend the range of class, like a patchwork in physical or social space.

Selection of Subjects
Once a particular locality is selected, contacts must be made with local leaders—school teachers, social workers, storekeepers, priests, local officials and politicians, teenage leaders—partly to learn about the way of life in the community, its aspirations and its sufferings, but also to locate the subjects for study. Through these local contacts, particular children are identified and met. Through these first children, once their confidence is gained, one meets their friends. Working through the existing social networks of local people and of

the children themselves, the investigators should choose a group of twenty children, equally divided between male and female. Not more than two children, one of each sex, should be chosen from the same household. The children should be aged twelve to fourteen years, but this age limitation may be varied in different cultures, and particularly between sexes, because of differentials in the rate of maturation between girls and boys. The intent is to reach subjects who are in early adolescence, at a time when they are no longer considered to be small children nor yet full-fledged adults. If the children are themselves organized in one or more "gangs" or other social groups, the process of study may be easier. In any event, they should preferably be known to each other and relatively at ease with one another.

A number of public officials should also be chosen for interviews, officials who make decisions that directly affect the development of children or of their spatial setting. They may be designers of housing, streets, or parks, be engaged in planning economic or physical development at the city or regional level, be concerned with planning and creating the regional system of education or child care, be local engineers, or political leaders. Ideally, these will be the officials who have been or are concerned with the locality in question, making recommendations or decisions that bear on the lives of the very children being studied. If this is not possible, the investigators should seek out those who work with similar areas or whose decisions might be influenced by the findings of the study. In the selection of officials for interview, as well as in the choice of locality, the local investigator should keep in mind the intent to connect findings with ongoing policy decisions.

Background Information

The survey teams should collect the following background information about the areas in which the behavior of children is being studied:
1. An outline base map of the area, which keys the locations of ground photographs and diagrams, names the principal features and the important land uses, and gives the scale and orientation. It should be possible to relate the image and action maps of the children to this base.
2. Vertical aerial photographs of the area, and stereo-pair coverage, if available. If they can be made, cheap paper enlargements of key photographs are very useful for annotation in the field, or as the basis for discussion.
3. Photographs taken from a sufficient number of points on the ground to make a systematic description of the character of all the different sections

of the area. Photographs should be taken at regular intervals (say, on a 100-meter grid) throughout the area, giving a characteristic view from the accessible outdoor space nearest to each grid intersection: street, open space, open lot, yard, waste area, or whatever. (See Figure 53 for a map of such a photographic grid.) In choosing his views from the grid point, the photographer should be alert to record children's activity, or such activity-related features as barriers, territorial markings, user modifications, symbolic identification, maintenance, or the scars of activity. Further photos may be necessary to explain special features, or to describe in detail elements that have proved to be important in children's behavior. The standpoint and direction of all ground photos should be keyed to a copy of the outline base map.

4. An outline map showing the relation of the area under study to the residential and work places of the people being observed (if elsewhere), as well as to the urban area, in general.

5. Old maps or photos that will help to illustrate how the area has changed, as well as any drawings that illustrate proposals for the future.

6. Simple plans of two or three typical interiors of the children's homes should be prepared. They may be freehand, and only roughly to scale, but should show typical room sizes, furniture locations, the foci of activity, and the density of occupation. The plans should be supplemented by verbal notes and by photographs of these interiors, if such may be taken without disturbance. Evidences of the children's activity, or their "territory," should be noted. Sketch plans, notes, and photos may possibly be made while interviewing children or parents in the home.

   In addition to background information on the setting, there should be background material on the parents and children being studied:

7. Their general socio-economic status, including sex, approximate age and income, occupation, caste and class or ethnic or religious group, formal education if any, and general health, as well as any apparent recent changes in income, occupation, or health.

8. A typical calendar of activity for these people and the usual timing of the day's activities for an adult. Length in residence in this locality and location of previous residence. The tenure of the space they occupy.

9. Any significant material available on prevalent attitude in this culture or subculture in regard to the development of children and their proper behavior in the physical environment. These may be in the form of references

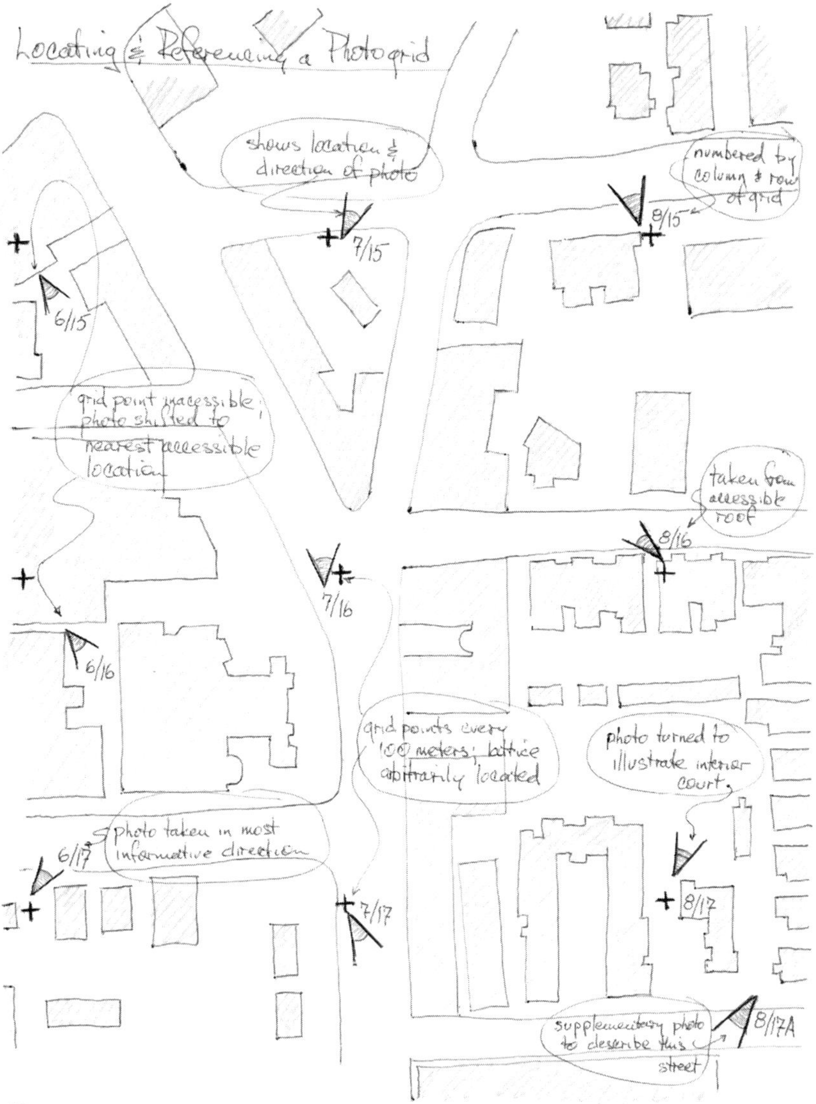
Locating & Referencing a Photogrid
shows location & direction of photo
numbered by column & row of grid
7/15
8/15
6/15
grid point inaccessible; photo shifted to nearest accessible location
taken from accessible roof
8/16
7/16
6/16
grid points every 100 meters; lattice arbitrarily located
photo turned to illustrate interior court
photo taken in most informative direction
6/17
7/17
8/17
supplementary photo to describe this street
8/17A

53
The example accompanying the guidelines, which illustrated how to generate and reference a photogrid.

to standard sociological or anthropological studies, or they may be novels, tales, songs, news clippings, jokes, drawings, and the like.
10. Finally, the analyst should refer to the official policies which directly influence the local physical environment of these children.

Analysis of Children's Image of Their Environment

This analysis is to consist of several actions to be carried out in this sequence: (1) making an acquaintance with the interviewees, and becoming familiar with the area and their mode of life; (2) individual interviews; (3) optional group discussions and guided tours.

Acquaintances and Orientation

After selecting the group to be studied, the local investigator must make their acquaintance, explain what the research is trying to discover and why, gain the children's assent to be studied, and come to easy terms with them. This can be expected to take time and to require some skill in human relations, plus the good offices of local community contacts. Initial distrust and shyness may be normal. The study should not commence unless and until the children are at ease with the investigators, understand the general purpose of the research, and are willing to assist in it.

While this acquaintance is ripening, the investigators should make themselves familiar with the local area and its features, prepare their working base map, make their land use and photographic surveys, and observe enough of the children's mode of life so that they can conduct the interview and the systematic observation in a knowledgeable way.

Individual Interviews

When this has been completed, an individual interview should be conducted with each child. Preferably, it will be held in some private space, so that spectators and other children will not disturb the results. Nevertheless, it should not be held in such a manner or place as to frighten the child or put him on the defensive. Thus, it should be in the child's local territory, in a place familiar and comfortable to him. At least one interviewer should be known to him, and preferably there will be only one. The interview should be conducted informally. It may even prove necessary to hold the discussion on the street despite the serious disadvantages of interruption and confusion. It can be useful if the results of the interview are recorded on tape, but equipment may be lacking, or it might be too distracting. In that case, notes must be taken such as to capture not only the details but also the flavor of the discussion, including salient quotations. The interviewer must supply large sheets of paper for maps, and some chalk, easy-flowing pens, or soft pencils. All original drawings are to be preserved and transmitted intact, and not copied, corrected, or tidied-up. If made on slates or drawn on the earth, they should be photographed, or at least copied exactly, without change of style or "improvement." Since the final question refers to activities of the previous day, the interview date should be chosen so that the previous day would be likely to be a normal one in the child's life and not a holiday or other interruption.

The recommended interview consists primarily of a central "core," which should always be administered, since these particular questions have proved to be the most consistent sources of useful information. Following this "core," we describe a longer list of optional questions, some of which may be chosen for use according to particular interests. The local situation may suggest other situations as well. On no account allow the interview to become too long and exhausting for either party. The core will by itself provide a solid basis for analysis. The preferred order is as given, but the questions need not be followed rigidly, since some answers will appear that the interviewer should be ready to follow. Always pretest the interview with several similar children, and modify it accordingly, before using it with the selected group. Questions must not only be translated into the local language but almost always must be modified to make sense in the local culture.

The following questions are part of the "core":

1. Name, age, identification.
2. "How long have you lived here? Where did you come from before that?"
3. "Please draw me a map of the area you live in, and show me whatever you think is important in it." (While the child is making the map, the interviewer records the general sequence in which he makes it and notes interesting remarks or explanations.) If any elements of the map are obscure, the interviewer asks what they are and notes that explanation on the map. He then gives the child another color of pen or pencil and asks him, "Now show me on your map the places you do things in, or spend your time in, and the routes you travel along. Mark the areas that surround your area."

   (If he is unable to draw a map, ask him to make a verbal description, supplemented by drawing simple pictures, or by diagrams in the earth, etc. If an enlargement of an air photo is available, the child's account may refer to that, or an outline map may be used. But do not produce a map or photo for discussion until all other means have failed. Make an effort to persuade him to draw a map, since even the crudest diagram is very useful. Tell him that special skill is not expected. If necessary, show him crude maps of other places, but no official maps. Do not correct his work or ask him to do more than he does spontaneously. See Figures 29, 30, 31, 33, 35, 37, 39, 41, 43, 44 as examples of what may be expected.)

4. (After taking up the map), "Please write down for me a list of all the places you know of in your area, inside and outside." (When the child ceases to list, or after three minutes), "Now tell me in which of those places do you usually spend your time? What do you do there?" (Probe for a *detailed* account of what the child does there, instead of a generality such as "playing." In particular, how does he or she make use of the physical environment?) "Which of all those places you have named are the most important ones?" (Interviewer marks the child's list according to his answers, takes note of interesting remarks, then chooses one of the more important features, and asks), "How would you describe this place to someone who had never been there, and wanted to know what it was like to be there?"

5. "As you go about your usual day's activities, what particular places or things give you the most difficulty? Are there places where you get hurt, or have trouble, or can't do what you want to do? Are there places you can't get into, and wish you could? Are there any dangerous places in your area? What makes them dangerous?"

6. "Do you help maintain or fix up any part of your area? Does any part of it seem to belong to you? Are there places you feel like an outsider? Who owns the streets (or courtyards, or . . .) here, and who keeps them up (referring to the principal public spaces in the area)? Are there any places that nobody owns?"

7. "Where do you best like to be? Where do you least like to be? Where is the best place to be alone?"

8. "Has your area changed in your memory? Do you think it has become better or worse? Why? Have you been able to do anything to change it? What do you think will really happen to this place in the next ten years? Will you still be here? If not, where will you be?"

9. "Now please tell me about what you did all day yesterday, in detail: where you went, what happened, what you did, and the time you did it." (The interviewer should see that he gets a detailed, consecutive account, as accurately timed and located as possible. Together with the child, the investigator should record each event on a form that divides the day into half-hour

divisions. See Figure 23.) "Was there anything unusual about your activities yesterday? If so, what was it?"

These are the basic questions to be asked. They will produce an annotated map, an annotated list of places, a schedule of one day's events, the answers to questions 5 through 8, and the interviewer's notes on additional remarks. It is a reasonably long interview, and a break may be required. The questions cannot be followed rigidly, and the interviewer must always be ready to follow interesting leads. But this is the general order to be used.

Optional Interview Questions
In addition to this basic "core" of questions, there are a number of optional questions, *some* of which may be added to the basic list if they seem to fit local needs. Do not overload the interview, however. Too many questions will not only wear out the children but will produce more data than can be analyzed, much of it redundant. Only add a topic where the result will surely be relevant.

1. "Please draw me a map of the entire city and the whole region around it, as far as you know it. Show me all the important places in it, how to get around it, the places you have been to, and where your own area is."

2. "Please draw me a plan of your own home, your building, and your yard. Show me the places you use most."

3. "On what occasions do you go out of your own area? What for? Where? How do you get there? Do you go by yourself, or with someone else? Can you go wherever you want in the whole city? Where can't you go, and why not? When did you last go into an unfamiliar part of the city? How did you find your way?"

4. Photograph some dozen views of typical locations and activities in the child's area, inside and out, and add, perhaps, a few views taken elsewhere in the city. Display them one by one in random order and ask, "What place is this? What is happening there? Tell me something else about it? Do you use it, or go there? Do you like it, or dislike it? Why?"

5. Construct one or two simple line drawings showing children doing something in a setting—some action that is possible in the culture but can be interpreted in different ways, depending on the attitudes you are interested in—for example: children playing in a refuse dump (are they having fun, or are they in danger?), children helping to build a house (is it satisfying or is it drudgery?), children on a crowded bus (are they lost or having an

adventure?), children listening to a teacher in school (are they bored or interested?), and so forth. Display a drawing and ask: "Would you tell me a story about this picture?"

6. Put a large piece of paper on a smooth base, and give the child a box of three-dimensional scaled models of elements of the environment (buildings, trees, cars, people, etc.) which would be sufficiently typical to allow him to make a passable model of his area. Give him marking pens or crayons to draw in the fields, roads, etc. Ask, "Would you use these to make a model of the place you live in?" Photograph the result, or help the child to trace around all the three-dimensional elements, to make a permanent record of his model. Give him the scale figure of a child, and say, "Now, let's pretend this is yourself. Show me where you usually go during the day, what you do, who you meet, what happens." Note the sequence of events, the way in which the environment is used, the child's feelings, any salient remarks.

7. "Think of all the people that you know, and write their names down on this paper." When the child ceases to list, or after three minutes, "Now, go back over the list, and mark with (some symbol) all the ones who are your relatives or part of your family, all the ones who live in your area, and all who are children of about your age. Going back again, mark all those you usually meet at least once a day, the others that you meet more than once a month, and, finally, those you never meet or don't expect to meet again. Going back still again, mark those you usually meet at school, the others you usually meet in someone's home, those you meet outdoors (plus any other likely locale: work place, club, etc.). Finally, mark the ones you like." Optional addition, "Go down the list of those that live in your area, and show me on this map (or enlarged air photo) where each one lives, if you know."

8. "Are there beautiful places in the city? Why are they beautiful? Any holy places? Why are they holy?"

9. "Please tell me about the happiest day in your life, and where it happened. Now, tell me about the saddest one, and where it happened."

10. "Of all the places that you have ever been in, or heard about, or imagined, what would be the best place to live in? Why? Would you draw a picture of it for me? What would be the worst place you could imagine? Would you draw a picture of it?"

11. "What kind of weather is worst for you? Why? Do you ever find the air uncomfortable to breathe, or unpleasant to smell, or does it hurt your eyes?"

12. "Are there any animals or plants in your area that you particularly like or dislike? Do you use any of them for food, or make things out of them? Do you like to play with animals or insects? Are there any plants, animals, or insects in your area that are being harmed, and should be protected?"

13. "Tell me about the history of your area. What was it like before? Who lived there? What important things have happened there? Are there any historical places or monuments there, that you know of?"

14. "What new things have you learned about, while going about your area of the city, or while watching things happen there? What have you learned to do from working or playing there? Is this something you wouldn't learn at school, at home, or from TV?"

Optional Discussions and Tours

When the individual interviews are complete, the investigators may choose to go further by bringing together one or two groups of four to five children each for a freer discussion of how they use their space, what they like or dislike, what the differences are between them, and so on. Once the regular interviews have been completed and absorbed, the investigators should be ready to lead such a discussion by asking stimulating questions. Maps, sketches, aerial photos, and ground photographs of key features of the area may also be used as a basis of the discussion. The group would be chosen so as to be at ease with each other, but also to exhibit some contrasting attitudes, or ways of acting.

If the children express interest, the investigators may also take a group on a trip to some unfamiliar areas of the city. The children themselves can help to plan the trip, going to places they have never seen but have always wanted to see. Comments and actions during the trip could be noted, and a recorded group discussion about the experience should be held. Photographs should be taken on the trip of what interests the group, to be discussed at a later session.

An individual or a small group might take the investigator on a tour of their own familiar area, pointing out to him the various places they have talked about, and discussing their feelings about them. Still another useful technique is to give the children simple cameras, and ask them to take pictures of "things that interest them" in their area. These photos can be the basis of a group discussion, or can be the nucleus for a description and analysis of their area to be prepared as an exhibition by the children for use in school or by children in other areas.

54
The example accom-
panying the guide-
lines, showing a
behavioral diagram
with a suggested
legend.

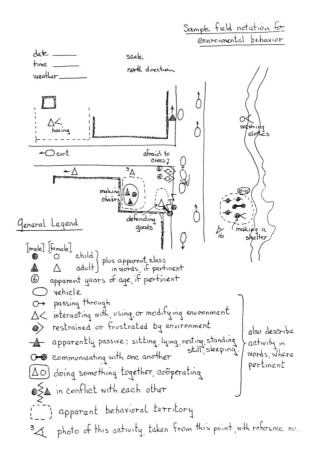

Sample field notation for
environmental behavior

Observations of Children's Spatial Behavior

After the individual interviews are complete, and while or after any group tours and discussions are taking or have taken place, the investigators should make a systematic record of visible child behavior in the open places of the area. For this purpose, they must first choose about four locales. These should be places that represent most of the important types of activity settings for children in the area: public thoroughfare, water supply point, garden, eating place, sleeping place, work place, meeting place, playground, etc. Each locale should be a place where a typical kind of activity recurs regularly, and the various locales should between them exhibit most of the visible outdoor behavior of children in the area.

On two normal days, and one normal holiday (a Sunday, for example), an analyst should visit each locale two or three times during the course of the day, and, if relevant, the night, the visits being timed to cover expected variations in activity. For each visit to each locale, he should note the time, the weather, and the general activity and type of people present, and which of them are similar in age and class to the interviewees.

The actions of this latter group should be described in some detail, recorded on a simple diagram supplemented with verbal notes and one or more photographs. This will give a clear and concrete picture and allow comparison with the interview results. Record should be made of which children are acting together, and which separately, and how they are using or being frustrated by the physical environment, as well as how it seems to modify their action (sitting on a fence, slipping in the mud, scavenging material, seeking shade, etc.). Gesture, voice, and manner can be noted. Instances of conflict or competition over space, or of the significance of territory or timing, should also be recorded (the police drive children off, children defend their place against invasion, they eat in a regular place at a regular time, etc.). Any adaptations of the physical space by the children should be noted (erecting a shade or rain shelter, marking boundaries, writing on walls or pavements, setting up furniture, levelling ground, etc.). The dynamic aspect must also be captured: how activity is changing, or where children are moving. (See Figure 54 for an example of a simple field notation for recording the visible activity of children in one locale at one time. The physical setting need only be shown where it is relevant to the action or needed to key in the photographs. This way of classifying activity should not simply be copied, however. Classification must arise out of the culture, and simply be as concrete and descriptive as possible.) At each visit, a photograph or photographs should be taken that illustrate the typical activity at that time. From his knowledge of the area, the analyst may also choose to make special comments, to note variations from routine, or to visit some other particular place at a special time. If it is possible to make, a motion picture or videotape record of the activity will be an excellent addition. It will be a dynamic, yet permanent, record which can later be studied in detail.

This material can now be summarized in a running account of the typical spatial behavior in these several places, with a commentary on how it compares with the picture derived from the interviews and group discussions, and how it illuminates any of the major themes of this study: spatial territory, the timing of activity, the way in which the spatial environment supports human inter-relations, its probable effect on child development and health, and the creation of reliable indices of environmental quality.

·The summaries and high points of interviews and group discussions, trans-lated into English, plus all original maps, diagrams, schedules, sketches (or at least *exact* copies of them), photographs, and field notations, should be trans-mitted along with the summary reports of the local team.

Analysis of the Knowledge, Attitudes, and Memories of Parents and Officials

At option, one parent may be interviewed for each child studied, and should preferably be of the same sex as that child. This may be a good opportunity to record the internal setting of the home. In addition to any questions required to supplement direct observation in order to establish social-economic status, residence, tenure, and time resource budgets (see questions 7 and 8 discussed under Background Information on page 86, but these questions should be mini-mal, informal, and come at the end of any interview), they should be asked the following:

1. "What part of the day or night does your child normally spend outside the home? In what places and at what hours? What does he/she do there? How often do you see him/her?"
2. "What did your child do yesterday, and where?" (in some detail)
3. "Are those places suitable for what he/she was doing, or how should they be changed?"
4. "Is any of this activity unsafe, or improper, or wasteful? Why? How would you prefer his time be spent? What could be done about it?"

5. "How much of the city does the child know, and how far does he/she go? Do you take him out into it? Where? How often? Why?"
6. "What does your child need most? What do you need to take care of your child?"
7. "How do you think your children's children will spend their time, and what will the places they live in be like? What do you wish those places could be?"
8. "Tell me about what it was like when you were a child—what do you remember of the place you lived in, and what did you do there? How does that compare with the place your child is growing up in today? Which place was better to grow up in and why?"

Summaries of each interview should be recorded, translated into English, and transmitted, along with a means of identifying the parent with the particular child.

Whether parents are or are not interviewed, a few officials whose decisions are relevant to the area should be contacted, in order to illuminate the policy implications of the study. See Selection of Subjects, page 84, for the criteria for choosing the officials to be interviewed. Each official should be interviewed to elicit:

1. His knowledge of how children in the area make use of it, that is, what they do, where, and at what times; the range and purpose of their activity; and how the environment supports or frustrates those purposes. Detailed questions on these matters can most easily be prepared after the analyst has a thorough understanding of how children are actually acting.
2. In the early course of the interview, the planner should be asked to make a sketch map of the area in question, as far as he knows it. Later, he might be asked to add any features in it (in another color) that appeared as significant in the discussion.
3. The planner's own evaluation of the quality of that micro-environment and how his official plans affect that quality, or are affected by it; and his sense of how the development of these children is affected by the micro-environment and the children's use of it.
4. Memories of his own childhood environment, and its evaluation in comparison with that of these area children (just as was asked of the children's parents).
5. His estimate of how that environment and its use by children is currently changing, and what he thinks the realistic environmental expectations may be for the next generation of children of this class.

6. A description of the data and criteria he commonly uses in planning for these children or for this or similar areas.

General Conclusions

The survey should conclude with comments on the following items. In addition, the local team should discuss any other issues relevant to our purposes, which the research has uncovered. Assertions founded on the data are to be distinguished from speculation, but informed speculation should not be excluded.

First, there must be some concise description of the physical setting: the spaces, shelters, circulation, natural features, and other elements important to the children's behavior.

Then should come a discussion of the principal factual findings on how these children use and image their micro-environment, including:

1. Their spatial range and the detailed spatial and temporal pattern of their activity. Where and when they eat, sleep, play, excrete, work, learn. How much of this occurs at home, at school, in the public outdoor space, elsewhere.
2. The extent to which they are able to do what they propose to do: how their activities are interrupted or blocked, how they adapt and "make do," what conflicts arise, what environmental dangers and discomforts they endure, what they have access to.
3. How they adapt the setting itself: what modifications they make, how they maintain the space, what controls they exercise.
4. Their attitudes about the environment: ideas of danger, pollution, discomfort, sacredness, beauty, utility, openness, crowding. How the environment reinforces their feelings of identity, territory, privacy, community. Their knowledge of the environment, how they learn from it, or teach others about it.
5. What they expect from the environment, and how those experiences are being met. Their hopes and desires for the future. What priority changes they would make in their surroundings, if they were able to do so. How the environment appears to stimulate, open up, or block various avenues of personal development.
6. How the child's actual spatial behavior compares with the parent's knowledge and evaluation of it, with the parent's expectations, and with the parent's own remembered childhood.

7. How the behavior compares with the knowledge and attitudes and child-hood of the various officials; and with the data that they customarily use. How child behavior is affected by official actions.

8. How present use and space is changing, and how the children's expectations compare with realistic expectations for the future.

9. What are the probable consequences of this way of life on the development and future usefulness of these children? Is the quality of the micro-environment in this regard improving or deteriorating? To what extent is this the result of official development decision? What seem to be the criti-cal qualities of the environment—density, access, territory, manipulability, pollution, shelter, whatever—that affect the health and development of these children?

And last, and most important:

10. What specific changes in policy can therefore be recommended—whether in regard to the micro-environment itself, or to environmental services, or to education, or to child care, or to other areas of public action—that would improve the health, personal development, and social usefulness of these children?

Selections from the Original Research Guide

We have extracted only those portions of the original guide that are necessary to correlate the first studies with the procedures originally recommended for them. Even so, the national teams made additions and modifications of their own, and variations on the original were also suggested by the scientific advisor in informal communication. This original guide was written in 1971 by Banerjee and Lynch. Even in extract form, much of it is necessarily a repetition of the full recommended guide discussed previously.

Individual Interviews

The following questions should be asked:

1. Name, age, identification.

2. "How long have you lived here? Where did you come from before that?"

3. "Where do you sleep, and where do you eat? What part of the day do you spend in a house, and what part outside? Do you go to school? Can you tell me what you do on a usual day, where do you do it and with whom?"

4. "Please draw for me a map of the area you live in. Show me: the places you do things in, or spend your time in, including the things you just talked

about; the routes you travel along; all the places you think are important in the area; and the other areas that surround your area." If he is unable to draw a map, ask him to make a verbal description, supplemented by pointing out the places, by drawing simple pictures, by diagrams in the earth, etc. If this is not explicit, and an enlargement of an air photo is available, the child's account may refer to that. But do not produce a map or photo for discussion until other means have failed. Make an effort to persuade him to draw a map, since even the crudest diagram is very useful. Tell him that special skill is not expected. If necessary, show him other crude maps of other places, but no official maps.

5. "What is the name of your area? How would you describe it to someone who had never been there and who wanted to know what it was like to be there?"

6. "What are the other areas that surround your particular area? Are they different from yours?" If yes, "How are they different?"

7. "On what occasions do you go out of your own area? What for? Where? How do you get there? Do you go by yourself?"

8. "Now, please draw me a map of the entire city. Show me: all the important places in it; how to get around in it; the places you have been to; the routes you have been on; and where your own area is."

9. "Can you go wherever you want in your own area? in the whole city? Where can't you go? Why not? Would you like to go there? How do you know about these places? Do your parents let you go where you like? Do they take you anywhere? Did anyone ever teach you how to get about in the city? Did you teach anyone? When did you last go into an unfamiliar part of the city? How did you find your way there?"

10. "As you go about your usual day's activities, what features in your area make the greatest difficulties for you—most hinder you? Where do you best like to be, and what do you do there? Where do you least like to be, and what do you do there? What would you like to do, but can't do? Where is the best place to meet your friends? Where is the best place to be alone?

11. "Where in your own area do you feel most at ease, "at home," most comfortable and like yourself and able to do what you want? Why? Does any part seem to belong to you, so that you control it? Are there places where you feel like an outsider? Are there places where you have to fight for space? Who owns the streets here, and who keeps them up? Are there any places that nobody owns?"

12. "Are there any dangerous places in your area? What makes them danger-ous? What is the most dangerous place in the whole city? Why?"

13. "Are there any beautiful places in the city? Why are they beautiful? Any holy places? Why?"

14. "Has your area changed in your memory? Do you think it has become better or worse? Why? What are the things you could do before but not anymore? What are the things that you couldn't do before but now you can? Have you been able to do anything to change it? How would you change the area if you could do anything you wanted to it? Would every-one here agree to that, or would some oppose it? What do you think should be changed here?"

15. "What do you think will really happen to this place in the next ten years? Will you still be here? If not, where will you be and how will you be living?"

16. "Of all the places that you have been in, or heard about, or imagined, What would be the best place to live in? Why? Could you describe it to me?"

17. "Please tell me about the happiest day in your life. Now tell me about the saddest one."

18. "Now, please tell me about what you did all day yesterday in some detail, who you saw, where you went, and what happened, including the time you did it, where, with whom, and how you got from one place to an-other." The interviewer should see that he gets a detailed, consecutive ac-count as accurately timed and located as possible. Together with the child, the investigator should record each event and its timing, at the correct lo-cation on an enlarged aerial photograph or on a copy of the base map. "Was anything unusual about your activities yesterday? If so, what was it?"

Group Discussions and Tours

When the individual interviews are complete, the investigators should bring to-gether one or two groups of four to five children each, for a freer discussion of how they use their space, what they like or dislike, what the differences are be-tween them, and so on. Once the regular interviews have been completed and absorbed, the investigators should be ready to lead such a discussion by asking stimulating questions. Maps, sketches, aerial photos, and ground photographs of key features of the area may also be used as a basis of the discussion. The group would be chosen so as to be at ease with each other, but also to exhibit some contrasting attitudes, or ways of acting.

If the children express interest, the investigators may also take a group on a trip to some unfamiliar areas of the city. The children themselves can help to plan the trip, going to places they have never seen but have always wanted to see. Comments and actions during the trip could be noted, and a recorded group discussion about the experience should be held. Photographs should be taken on the trip of what interests the group, to be discussed at this later session.

Observations of Spatial Behavior

After the individual interviews are complete, and while or after group tours and discussions are taking or have taken place, the investigators should make a systematic record of the visible behavior in the open places of the area. For this purpose, they must first choose about six locales; that is, places that are easily visible and that represent all the important types of activity settings for children in the area: public thoroughfare, water supply point, garden, eating place, sleeping place, work place, meeting place, playgrounds, etc. Each locale should be a place where a typical kind of activity recurs regularly, and among them the locales should exhibit most of the visible outdoor behavior of children in the area.

On two normal days, and one normal holiday (a Sunday, for example) and one special holiday, an analyst should visit each locale two or three times during the course of the day, and, if possible, once at night, the visits being timed to cover expected variations in activity. For each visit to each locale, he should note the time, the weather, and the general activity and type of people present. In particular, he should describe the actions of the children who are there, and who are similar in age and class to the interviewees.

Their actions should be described in some detail to give a clear and concrete picture and to allow a comparison with the interview results. Notes should be made of which children are acting together, and which separately, and how they are using or being frustrated by the physical environment, as well as how it seems to modify their actions (sitting on a fence, slipping in the mud, scavenging material, seeking shade, etc.). Instances of conflict or competition over space, or of the significance of territory or timing, should also be recorded (the police drive the children off a street, children defend their sleeping place against invasion, they eat in a regular place at a regular time, etc.). Any adaptations of the physical space by the children should be noted (erecting a shade or rain shelter, marking boundaries, writing on walls or pavements, setting up furniture, levelling ground, etc.). At each visit, a photograph or photographs should be taken that illustrate the typical activity at that time. From his knowledge of the area, the analyst may also choose to make special comments, to note variations from routine, or to visit some other particular place at a special time.

This material can now be summarized in a running account of the typical spatial behavior in these several places, with a commentary on how it compares with the picture derived from the interviews and group discussions and how it illuminates any of the major themes of this study: spatial territory, the timing of activity, the way in which the spatial environment supports human interrelations, its probable effect on child development and health, and the creation of reliable indices of environmental quality.

Interviews and group discussions, translated into English, plus all original maps, diagrams, sketches (or at least *exact* copies of them), photographs, and field notations, should be transmitted with the summary report of the local team.

The Analysis of the Attitudes and Memories of Parents
One parent should be interviewed for each child studied and should, preferably, be of the same sex as that child. In addition to any questions required to supplement direct observation in order to establish social-economic status, residence, tenure, and time resource budgets, they should be asked the following:
1. "What part of the day or night does your child normally spend outside the home? In what places and at what hours? What does he/she do there? How often do you see him/her?"
2. "What did your child do yesterday, and where?" (in some detail)
3. "Are those places suitable for what he/she was doing, or how should they be changed?"
4. "Is any of this activity unsafe, or improper, or wasteful? Why? How would you prefer his time be spent? What could be done about it?"
5. "How much of the city does the child know, and how far does he/she go? Do you take him out into it? Where? How often? Why?"
6. "What does your child need most? What do you need to take care of your child?"
7. "How do you think your children's children will spend their time, and what will the places they live in be like? What do you wish those places could be?"
8. "Tell me about what it was like when you were a child—what do you

remember of the outdoors in the place you lived in, and what did you do there? How does that compare with the place your child is growing up in? Which place was better to grow up in and why?"

The detailed results of each interview should be recorded, translated into English, and transmitted, along with a means of identifying the parent with the particular child.

The Analysis of the Attitudes, Knowledge, and Plans of Official Environmental, Education, and Child Care Planners

Each planner should be interviewed to elicit:

1. His knowledge of how children in the area use the outdoor space: that is, what they do, where, and at what times; the range and purpose of their activity; and how the environment supports or frustrates those purposes. Detailed questions on these matters can most easily be prepared after the analyst has a thorough understanding of how children are actually acting.
2. In the early course of the interview, the planner should be asked to make a sketch map of the area in question, as far as he knows it. Later, he might be asked to add any features to it (in another color) that appeared as significant in the discussion.
3. The planner's own evaluation of the quality of that micro-environment and how his official plans affect that quality, or are affected by it; and his sense of how the development of these children is affected by the micro-environment and the children's use of it.
4. Memories of his own childhood environment, and its evaluation in comparison with that of these area children (just as was asked of the children's parents).
5. His estimate of how that environment and its use by children is currently changing, and what he thinks the realistic environmental expectations may be for the next generation of children of this class.
6. A description of the data and criteria he commonly uses in planning for this or similar areas.
7. A description of any existing or proposed program for children of this kind which the planner is aware of.

This verbal and sketch data should be recorded and transmitted in detail, the verbal material being translated into English, as necessary.

EXCERPTS FROM THE NATIONAL REPORTS

The work of each local team is systematically covered in reports that are available for consultation at the Applied Social Sciences Division of UNESCO in Paris. Each report is complete in itself. We will not attempt to summarize their findings here. That was done in an impressionistic way in the main text. Rather, we will choose fragments that give a better sense of the localities that were studied, or communicate some interesting findings.

Australia

We begin with the Melbourne study, conducted by Peter Downton, and completed in 1973.[1] It dealt with eleven girls and nine boys, aged fourteen to fifteen, living in the western suburbs of Melbourne, Australia.

The western suburbs of Melbourne are generally of a lower status socially, economically and in terms of physical facilities than those to the east of the C.B.D. There are many social indicators supporting this assertion: The average per capita expenditure on new education buildings 1966-1972 throughout Melbourne was $257; the western suburbs averaged $138. The per capita value of new health building approvals for the year ending 6/30/1971 for all areas of Melbourne other than the Inner Western sector averaged $3.87; for the Inner Western sector the value was $0.14. The west continually ranks low on such indicators, hence it was decided to choose a particular area within this sector as our study area. It was considered that such a study might prove of value in helping to improve conditions in these suburbs.

Jointly, the city councils of the suburbs of the Western sector of Melbourne are making submissions to the Federal Government for assistance in improving conditions in the area.

Against this background the areas of Braybrook and Maidstone were chosen for the study. The area is within the City of Sunshine. It has considerable industrial development, a high usage of land for governmental purposes, and a residential layout substantially similar to the Australian norm. It has larger blocks of land than those found in most suburbs. The houses throughout are public authority erected, a high proportion being rented. The area was established in the late 1940s and early 1950s and has four distinct types of house— prefabricated timber, prefabricated concrete, brick-veneer attached pairs, and timber units for railways employees. There are also a number of prefabricated concrete flats of up to three storeys and a few similar blocks of brick flats. [pages 1-2] [2]

• • •

[1] Reported in: P. J. Downton, "Children's Perception of Space Project; Melbourne Study," typescript, March 1973.

[2] Page numbers following quoted material refer to the respective national reports.

55
Aerial view of the
Braybrooke-Maidstone
area in Melbourne.
The Maribyrnong is to
the north (top) of the
photo, beyond the
screen of factories.
Note the frequent,
empty, public open
spaces.

The children were mainly fourteen, and in the third year of their secondary schooling. They thus fitted the criteria of being in early adolescence, and of an age when they are no longer considered as small children, nor yet adults in their community. Children must compulsorily remain at school until the age of fifteen by State Law. Many of these children are likely to be leaving school in 1973 to find employment, at which stage (and a little older) they can expect to be treated in a more adult fashion. At the age studied they are expected to take responsibility for some household duties (e.g., tending younger children in the family), but are also expected to behave according to parental demands which limit their degree of self-determined behaviour. [page 10]

. . .

The City of Melbourne (Lat. 37°49'S, Long. 144°58'E) lies at the northern end of a large shallow bay. The area of the existing urban zones is 1,380 square kilometres with an estimated population of 2.5 million people. To the west and north lie flat basalt plains, and through this area runs the Maribyrnong River. The average annual rainfall of this western sector is 500·mm. The mean maximum annual temperature is 19°C., the mean minimum annual temperature is 9°C., while the mean maximum monthly temperature in summer is approximately 27°C., and for winter months the mean monthly minimum is approximately 4.5°C. During the period of the study the maximum daily temperature averaged 18°C. The rainfall was insignificant as the area was experiencing drought conditions. [page 14]

. . .

An average street could be described as consisting of a paved central section, usually of bitumen, but occasionally concrete, edged with concrete (or occasionally bluestone block) drainage channels. This centre roadway is flanked on either side by a poorly maintained area of grass. Implanted in the grass are timber poles carrying power and telephone lines. Very rarely a small tree may also be found in this area which is usually named (in one of the great Australian misnomers) the "nature strip." Between the nature strips and the front fences on either side of the street there are concrete footpaths. The distance between the front fences is in the order of 16-19 m in most instances.

The front fences are typically very low and serve only as demarcation lines, keeping nothing in or out. The front walls of the houses are set some 6 or 8 metres behind these fences. In the older parts of the West Footscray section this distance is frequently less. The area between the front fence and the house is relatively useless as it lacks privacy for quiet uses, and is too small for more vigorous activities. Often an attempt is made to make this area ornamental.

The houses are set about 3.5 metres from one side boundary to allow for a drive and/or garage for cars and a little over a metre from the other boundary. The space between the rear of the house and the fence dividing the block from the one backing onto it forms a more or less visually private outdoor space [page 151] (See Fig. 2.)

. . .

The parks and reserves in the area may generally be described as flat, feature-less tracts of haphazardly grassed unused land. They inevitably appear larger than they are, an illusion resulting from boredom. Several of them have trees in a line along one or more sides. One park has trees toward the centre. The football club and the schools in the area have similar reserves, the differences being the addition of a two metre high wire mesh fence around the periphery topped with barbed wire, and a strict absence of trees. [page 20] (See Fig. 3.)

• • •

The land south of the Maribyrnong River is a cross between a wilderness and a rubbish dump. It grades steeply to the river. On the north side the land is com-paratively flat beside the river before rising steeply. This flat area is well used for riding horses, fishing, walking, etc. Some swimming takes place in the river, but many feel it to be too polluted now to be safe. [page 23]

• • •

Nearly all journeys undertaken within the study area by fourteen year olds are by foot. Some journeys to and from school are by bus, a few by car, but most by foot. Bicycle riding is very limited as a means of movement for this age group. Motor bike riding for fun is quite common, but is illegal on roadways so it is not used much for transport. The interviews have constant mentions of walking to visit friends. Observations in the area revealed large numbers of boys and girls in the 13 to 17 age group walking around the streets in groups of from two to six. Larger sustained groups were not common except for those walking home from school.

Two-thirds of the children interviewed consider themselves able to go wherever they wish in both their own area and in the city. Typically, there are conditions imposed by parents, such as a time by which the child must return, or the stipulation that the child must say where he or she proposes to go. The remainder of the subjects either feel considerable limitations, or definitely say that there are a number of places where they cannot go. The children are often limited to going to places they already know. This typically applies to journeys to the city, where many children are not allowed without company.

"Can't go to the city unless I'm with Mum. I don't know the city, I've only been once in the last three years."

The same girl provided a fairly typical answer when asked if she was able to go wherever she wanted in her own area.

"I can go where I want to provided I tell Mum, and there is somebody with me."

Telling Mum is the operative condition for most of the respondents. Journeys that involve long distances, and hence public transport, are limited for many by money. This was not often mentioned in answer to this question, but be-came evident somewhere in the interview.

In several instances the limitations governing which places are accessible come from the child rather than the parents. The following is typical: when asked if she could go wherever she wanted in the city, one girl replied—

"Yes, but I don't like going into the city by myself—I could go with Vicki, but we don't know the way and would get lost."

The range of places specifically disallowed by the parents is fairly narrow. Billiard rooms and hotels are mentioned by many. All subjects are of course several years too young to be legally served in a hotel. Picture theatres showing "R" certificate films are mentioned by several. ("R" certificate specifies that children under eighteen years of age shall not be admitted.) Places considered physically dangerous were mentioned infrequently in answer to these questions. Whirlpools in the river, and main roads were both cited as places where two boys could not go in their area. [pages 26-28]

• • •

Because it quickly became obvious that most activity by this age group in public space took place in the streets, we began observing streetscapes. The activity in the streets was based on walking and meeting people, hence it rarely occurred in the same location twice. Consequently, it was necessary for the observation team to drive around looking for the action.

To remain inconspicuous, photos were taken with long telephoto lenses from within the car.

The following sketches and notes explain the uses of space observed. No real modification of the environment was observed. Various environments were being used in ways for which they were not intended—the steps in front of the squash courts as seats, front fences as seats, streets as cricket grounds, etc. Making tracks by riding bikes over unused ground is the nearest action we observed to genuine modification of a space. [page 31]

• • •

Most children seem to desire to use these areas (the reserves) for activities specifically banned by Councils—horse, push bike and motor bike riding, flying model planes and kites, digging, building, climbing, etc. By removing these potential users of the provided open space the reserves are left empty and lifeless.

Use of space outside the house lot by children is predominantly confined to the streets. Young children play in the streets because they provide the only near-to-home public space large enough for the energetic games. Children around the age we studied use the streets in an essentially social manner—to walk and watch, to be seen, to meet friends and to gather and talk.

Although this use of space is not regarded as very bad or wrong by parents, they are not particularly happy about it. Short of keeping the children inside, they seem powerless to alter this behaviour pattern. [page 61]

• • •

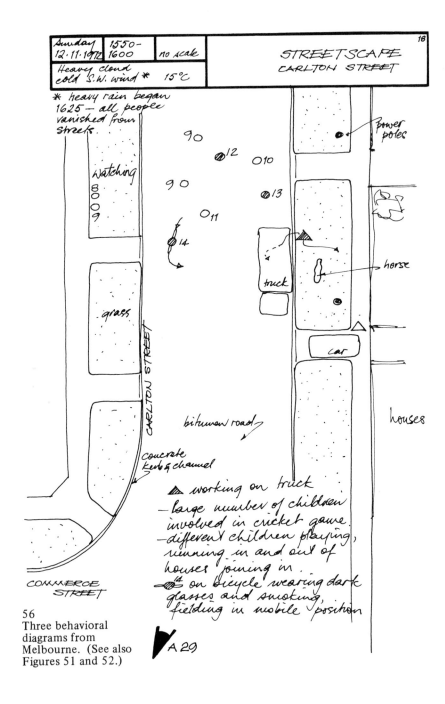

Sunday 12·11·1972	1550– 1600	no scale		STREETSCAPE CARLTON STREET
Heavy cloud cold S.W. wind *	15°C			

18

* heavy rain began 1625 — all people vanished from streets.

90

@12   O10

Watching
8
0
9

90

@13

O11

14

power poles

truck

horse

car

houses

CARLTON STREET

grass

bitumen road

concrete kerb & channel

COMMERCE STREET

◢ working on truck
— large number of children involved in cricket game.
— different children playing, running in and out of houses joining in.
14 on bicycle wearing dark glasses and smoking, fielding in mobile position

▶ A 29

56
Three behavioral diagrams from Melbourne. (See also Figures 51 and 52.)

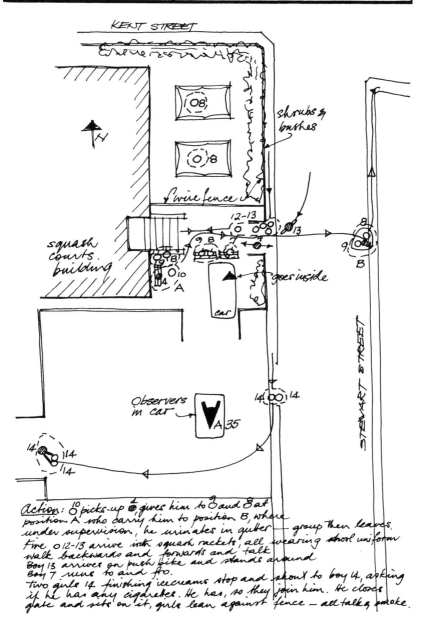

Monday 13.11.1972	1615–1625	1:800	SQUASH COURTS
Cloudy occassional hazy sun, light S.W. wind		16°C	FRONT ENTRY & CAR PARK

KENT STREET

08

0 8

shrubs & bushes

wire fence

12-13

13

8

9

B

squash courts building

9 8 7

8

10

4   A

goes inside

car

Observers in car

A 35

14   14

14

14

14

STEWART STREET

Action: 10 picks-up 2 gives him to 6 and 8 at position A who carry him to position B, where under supervision, he urinates in gutter — group then leaves.
Five 012-13 arrive with squash rackets, all wearing school uniform walk backwards and forwards and talk
Boy 13 arrives on push bike and stands around
Boy 7 runs to and fro.
Two girls 14 finishing icecreams stop and shout to boy 14, asking if he has any cigarettes. He has, so they join him. He closes gate and sits on it, girls lean against fence — all talk & smoke.

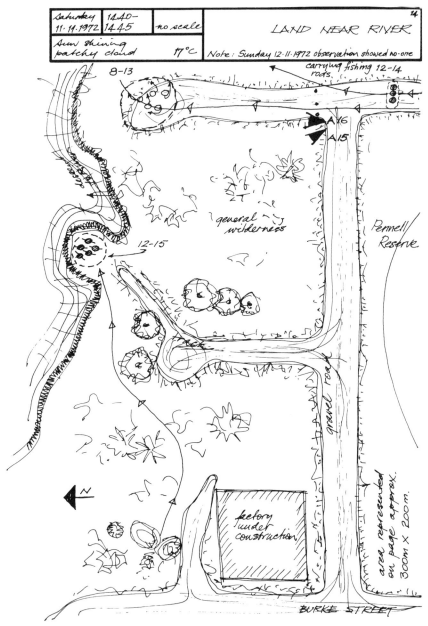

| Saturday 11·11·1972 | 14.40– 14.45 | no scale | LAND NEAR RIVER |
| Sun shining patchy cloud | 17°C | Note: Sunday 12·11·1972 observation showed no-one carrying fishing rods. |

14

8–13

A16
A15

carrying fishing 12–14 rods.

general wilderness

Pennell Reserve

12–15

gravel road

N

area represented on page approx. 300m × 200m.

factory under construction

BURKE STREET

Roads are clearly seen as the most dangerous places in the area. In one form or another, roads, intersections and heavy or fast traffic were mentioned eleven times. Ballarat Road running through the northern section of the study area is a major state highway and carries a large volume of traffic at all times. The children's school is beside this road and is reached by an overpass. It was specifically mentioned, as were other roads with heavy traffic. Some children simply specified roads in general.

The river is also seen as dangerous by some, being mentioned four times. Sometimes this is simply because it is a river and presents dangers such as whirlpools or falling in. The fact that "louts hang around there" also makes it dangerous. Only two replies mention this, but it is the general reputation of the river area at night.

Some mention the railway lines as dangerous. The lines run at the top of an embankment and are not fenced off. Train speeds are often high as there are major state lines as well as suburban lines.

The streets at night particularly near the football club are considered dangerous by about a quarter of the sample. Several parents also spoke of the streets as dangerous, the reasons given being invariably gangs and fights. Hotels, clubs, discotheques, billiard rooms, etc. are cited as places that might be dangerous because of gangs or fights.

The remainder of the answers seem, in the main, to result from some experience of the individual. One girl considers drains dangerous as her young cousin fell into one. Another expressed a fear of being pushed off the platform at a railway station. One boy itemized the most dangerous places in the whole city. The list comprises a lead pit, a shot tower, two chemical plants, and a creek with quick-sand. One boy informed the interviewer that the farm across the river was the most dangerous place "because you'd be shot if caught stealing carrots." The interviewer believed this was a rumour, not something the boy had experienced.

One girl gave the most general description for the most dangerous place.

"Anywhere—anything can happen to you!"

She gave the reason as:·

"Hoods—people out to get you. You can't be safe anywhere really! People jump out at you in the dark!" [pages 31-32]

· · ·

Questioned as to whether there were any beautiful places in the area or the city, sixteen children mentioned gardens, parks or anywhere with trees. Mainly this is outside their own area. (For the reason, see the treeless photos of the area.) One boy mentions a waterfall along the river (well out of the study area), and the city square in Melbourne is mentioned twice. This is wishful thinking for one subject, while to the other it is beautiful because you can watch people passing. There was one "don't know any," and one "there aren't any!"

Factories are the most frequently named "ugly places," being mentioned nine times. Poor houses in the area, pollution (especially near the river) and dumped rubbish and city buildings are each cited five times as examples of ugliness. One subject mentions old houses in an inner city area. One girl does not think anything is particularly ugly, ". . . everything's pretty much the same." Two boys said "No." Some ideas on ugliness:

"There are lots of houses unfit for living. The houses aren't looked after; you can look through the open doors and see mess and beer bottles everywhere."

"All round is ugly—it's a slum. The houses aren't looked after; people haven't got much money; places aren't sewered."

"Pennell's factory. It's not painted or kept tidy. It's old and rusty."

This factory was given as an example several times. Factories in general were usually mentioned although sometimes particular factories were singled out for attention. City buildings are, in the main, disliked because they are cold, tall, and concrete. [pages 32-33]

· · ·

For three children, their own room is the best place to be because they can pursue a hobby without interruption. Three others regard home generally as the best place to be, although one qualifies this by specifying that this is so only when his father is not home.

Another three children find a friend's home is the best place, one because she is free of her little brother, one because there are more things to do at her boyfriend's house, and one because she is getting away from her own home.

For one boy, who plays in a band with his father, the hotels where they play are best because all their friends are there. Another boy (who initially specified his own room) thinks anywhere he can go to fish is a good place.

Ten children all specify a sporting/social centre of some description as the best place to be, because they like the activity and they meet their friends there. The range is very wide and the emphasis is predominantly on the social nature of the activity.

In the light of the answer to the next question one girl surprisingly regards school as the best place because all her friends are there.

School is specified seven times as the least liked place, home twice, and both school and home once. For two girls there is nowhere that they object to enough to answer the question. Each of the other eight answers are unique:

In jail (the boy spent two days in police custody after stealing a car)

Sunshine—because there is nothing to do there

Doing a paper round—because it is boring, but he needs the money

The City—because the girl gets lost there

Aunt's home—because the boy had to work there

Inner suburbs—because there are "rotten old houses" there which are not interesting

Shopping—no reason

Church—". . . because the priest is always talking about wanting more money. Also it's all so boring." [pages 34-35]

. . .

Only one boy in the whole sample considers that he has been able to do anything to change the area. He has planted trees, mowed the lawn, and generally cared for the park directly opposite his house (Mathews Hill Reserve).

Asked how they would change the area if given a free hand most of the children gave extremely limited answers in keeping with their obviously limited experience. A fair composite answer would be: Plant more trees, improve the roads, pull down the flats, pull down all the factories and fix the place up generally. [page 42]

. . .

The children were asked their views on how the area would change in the next ten years. One girl believed there would be no real changes:

"I don't think it will change. There's nothing really to change in this area to make it different. There'll be different nationalities around, more road accidents especially around Darnley Street and Churchill Avenue corner, more crowding because there are so many people as the population is growing and hardly any places for them to live."

The rest believed there would be changes, some that it would get better, others that it would worsen, although half just thought there would be change and did not offer comment on whether this would improve or harm the area.

Most of those who expected some worsening of conditions mentioned crowding, pollution, noise, smells, and traffic.

Many expected that families of different nationalities would increasingly occupy the area. Some believed that conditions would be improved with better facilities, improved buildings and services. Several simply told of what they knew of proposed plans for the area—a new shopping complex to the northeast, one of the Catholic schools to become co-educational, etc.

Only three of the subjects expect to still be living in the area in another ten years, seven expect to be living somewhere similar or in a similar manner. The remainder hope to be somewhere else, particularly in the countryside away from the pollution, or near the city in a flat. There appears to be a strong desire to repeat the parents' pattern, with some improvements. The desire to live away from the metropolis will probably have to be modified by most because of a lack of job opportunities. The expressed desire by some to live near the city proper is usually dependent on a hoped for job or educational opportunity. Some suggest alternatives similar to their parents' pattern if such hopes are not fulfilled. One girl hoped to be living differently in Europe: ". . . there'll be trees and that!"

Most of the children interviewed regarded the abolition of flats as a desirable step in improving the environment. The Council and the Director of Welfare Services regard the introduction of flats as desirable. All those interviewed hope to see fewer, better controlled factories in the area in the future. The children's expectations for the future do not match well with the likely future.

The children's dislike of flats can be partially attributed to the general national dislike of flat living, and partially to the extremely poor quality of the flats in the area. Those children who live, or have lived, in one of the Housing Commission's concrete walk-up flats in the area understandably hate them. The lack of space within the flat, the lack of privacy, the featureless paddocks that separate individual blocks, and the depressing atmosphere of these developments are all aspects thoroughly disliked by both children and adults.

The following question was asked: "Of all the places that you have been to or heard about, or imagined, where would be the best place to live and why?"

Fifteen children named specific places. Six had actual experience of the place, and nine had heard about it. The other five each named a generalized type of place, three from experience.

Each place named is an extreme contrast to their own areas. European countries received five mentions, England twice, Sweden, Germany and Switzerland. Northern cities or areas of Australia were popular—Brisbane, Townsville, Queensland, Darwin, Bundaberg, The Gold Coast and "the outback" were mentioned once. Canberra was mentioned twice, as was the state of Tasmania. The beach or seaside and the countryside were mentioned several times each. Two rural centres, Wangaratta and Geelong, were named and so were two Melbourne suburbs, Rockbank and Toorak. (The latter is perceived as the suburb with the highest status.)

A place with trees, a lack of pollution, a free atmosphere, a smaller, more peaceful place, a clean and tidy place seems to be most desirable to the children. [pages 42-44, 57]

. . .

Parents were asked to try and describe the sort of place in which their grandchildren would live, both realistically, and in terms of their hopes for their children's children. Half the answers contained, either overtly or implicitly, the parents expectation that their children would repeat their suburban pattern with improvements. The improvements were either economic, social, or both. Several hoped there would be better community facilities. Many thought there would be more flats, but expressed hope that there would not be. Several answers, some entirely, some only partially, were restatements of the children's own hopes, and the parents admitted this.

Nearly all the answers contain reference to social conditions expected or hoped for in the future—usually in the form of "decent" living conditions, jobs, etc. Several said that their children's futures were dependent on their chances of pursuing their chosen careers.

Some sample answers are more illuminating than further analysis:

"I'd prefer her to get a better start than I did. I'd help her financially at the beginning. I think she'll have a clean, homely and happy house and be just like her mother—bored, overworked and housebound. I don't think she'll live too far from the city, but in a residential area, not an industrial one. I'd like the place to be like Beaumaris, near the beach. I'd want it to be a better environment than it is here. It'd have to be a decent place—it's so hard to be decent people otherwise. We've had to be strict in such a troublesome area, and it's very hard. Especially when she says, 'Well my friends are allowed to do that.' I'd prefer her to buy a block of land and save to build a house together."

"Places for Dawn will be further out of the city—places like Melton. If she's going to live a suburban life, I can't see her living in too crowded a place, such as flats. She'll be further out into the country, it'll be the only alternative for the future. I don't think she'll sit around and vegetate—she'll find things to do—she'll be a useful person in community activities. She'll have her own house, probably more spacious than this one—Jennifer and Dawn share the bedroom and I think Dawn feels the pinch a bit."

"Well, I hope what I've said is the sort of place she'll live in, where she'd got space to bring up her children—children need a backyard and need to make some noise—flats don't allow for this. The country is an ideal place. As you probably can tell, I was a country girl myself and I'd much rather live there. Although I'd like her to live in a residential area, not an area like this one."

"We get it rammed down our throats by the newspapers that the western suburbs are deprived, illiterate and breed crime and are full of no-hopers. Although this is not necessarily so, if you live in an area you're lumped with it. I don't think it's affecting her now, but if she has her choice later on it'd be better not to live here. It'd be easier on her." [pages 46-48]

· · ·

[The planners who were] interviewed described, usually at some length, childhoods that were the exact antithesis of a Braybrook childhood. Three of the architects grew up in the country areas which presented a wide range of activities and choices. Both Mr. O'Neill and Mr. Benjamin lived in urban areas which fortuitously provided them with equally varied spatial environments. All felt their childhoods were better. [page 54]

· · ·

The effect of the physical environment on these children is primarily one of limiting their experiences severely. The paucity of perceptual stimuli can be judged from the photographic descriptions of the area. Whether or not this inhibits the child's cognitive mapping, spatial learning and creative abilities cannot be judged accurately without a comparative study of other environments.

The range of experiences available to a child in the area is distinctly limited, shown in previous sections of this report. The chances for self-development, broadening of outlook, and contact with a variety of people and ideas are all very poor, hence the ability of the child to diverge from the pattern set by parents and the area subculture is limited. This lack is aggravated by a lack of educational opportunities. The resultant inhibited thinking of the children was extremely evident in the interview. [pages 61-62]

· · ·

This study has revealed that there is one primary fault in the outdoor public space in the study area. It is boring. This was clearly seen during photography and film making in the area. The film was made during school holidays, and everywhere we went within the area an audience of children quickly materialized. We made a point of asking these children (of various ages) what were their activities for the day, or during their holiday time. Inevitably, the replies were along the following general lines:

"Nothing much. Just messing around, there's nothing else to do."

The interview results reveal the same sense of boredom, although here, the social, physical, and educational environments can each be seen to be lacking interest for the children. The absence of creativity and invention in the thinking and use of time and space by these children is most noticeable, and the apparently unavoidable conclusion is that this is directly traceable to the lack of experiences, challenges and opportunities available in the social, physical and educational environments.

The present density of population has dictated the land of services and facilities, and the size of catchment areas for these facilities. The access to these facilities, given that ability to pay for transport remains unaltered, is affected by density. If the population is increased and at least the same level of services and facilities is maintained per head of population, the physical distances travelled to reach given facilities can be expected to decrease. Thus for children who predominantly walk, the access would improve.

Increased density may improve both access and manipulability in another way. An increase in population can be expected to lead to an increase in Council revenue from rates. Thus more money would become available for expenditure on services and facilities provided at a municipal level.

The children's access to usable outdoor public spaces is about half what it should be according to the Melbourne and Metropolitan Board of Works open space standards. However, these spaces are rendered almost unusable for children by lack of development on the one hand, and restrictions limiting their use to polite activities only on the other—walking, standing and talking are allowed and some sport (within rigid definitions of what constitutes sport).

There are only two interesting open spaces in the area—the railway land and the land adjacent to the river, and access to these is extremely limited. The position of both these places limits the access. Possible dangers limit access to the river further, and to use the railway land the children must trespass. During the time we were filming in the area the children were removed from their mini-bike track on the railway land by rail police. Some children were beginning to make use of a large empty site adjacent to a factory about 3.5 kilometres away (outside the study area). Their tenure of this site may well be limited and access is poor for children who previously used the railway land.

Access to outdoor space and other facilities could well improve due to new zoning. Unless these spaces are improved, access to them will remain pointless.

With the exception of the railway land and the land beside the river, the manipulability of the public open space is very close to zero. It is to be hoped that future planning within the area will go some way toward rectifying this. There appears to have been few attempts at improvement made in the past.

At present, pollution in all forms is a major element of the environment in the study area. It is a difficulty to be overcome if the land between the river and Ballarat Road is to be developed for recreational use. The condition of the Maribyrnong River and its immediate surrounds is a State concern. The factories providing air, water and visual pollution are also of concern to municipal authorities, as are the people who dump rubbish in the area. [pages 69-72)

• • •

The value of this and possible future similar studies is indicated by the interest aroused by the project in Melbourne.

Other researchers have been interested in such work, and hopefully some will direct this enthusiasm into similar or complementary research to increase the body of knowledge about the interaction between man and his built environment.

The project can be expected to give valuable indication of the influence of cultural differences on spatial use and behaviour. The application of findings from another country to planning or design problems is always accompanied by doubts as to the validity of such findings for local conditions. The clarification of cross-cultural differences and similarities is of primary importance in countries such as Australia where research in this field is severely limited and hence reliance on research in other countries is necessary.

Perhaps the most encouraging aspect of this project in Melbourne has been the interest expressed by planning authorities. They seek information urgently, and this highlights the primary weakness of the study. Planners and designers require information in a usable form, a form that allows simple synthesis of the information into a design decision, or planning solution or strategy. The information produced is not in such a form, nor is it statistically sound enough to be used confidently as a basis for decision making. It does, however, lead to a degree of enlightenment by indicating both tendencies in behavioural patterns of a particular group, and areas suitable for future research. [pages 68-69]

• • •

Argentina

The Argentinian study, completed in 1972, was conducted by Dr. Antonio M. Battro and architect Eduardo J. Ellis in the provincial city of Salta, in the extreme northwest of the country.[1] Nine boys and eleven girls aged eleven to fourteen were chosen for the study, all of whom lived in the residential suburb of Villa Las Rosas.

Villa Las Rosas is a suburb of the city of Salta. Construction commenced in 1954 to house persons in the lower middle class, with an average monthly income of US$ 70. The installments to purchase these lodgings consisted of loans from the Federal Mortgage Bank (Banco Hipotecario Nacional) with long term amortization and a low annual interest rate. Villa Las Rosas is located in the Southern zone of Salta and is accessible by one of the avenues (Irigoyen Ave.) with a dividing waterway along the axis. Its boundaries are clearly marked: the aforementioned avenue to the West, low hills to the East and South, and the Prison and the National Shooting Range (Tiro Federal) to the North.

Villa Las Rosas does not have a shopping center, as the school was erected in its place. The school is no doubt the center of many activities of this area.

Food shops have sprung up spontaneously from some private homes, using existent rooms or enlarging the original house for this purpose. In the case of enlargement the existing architectural unity disappears.

The streets are named after flowers, and the principal one, The Lilacs (Las Lilas) begins at Irigoyen Ave. (See Figs. 1 and 58.) The Lilacs is the main access to this area. An iron arcade with the suburb's name on it and a commercial sign mark the entrance portico. Next to the arcade is the church. The road ends up the hill, bypassing the school and the plaza. A Christmas show is given every year on the hillside, lasting ten days, with the children of the area participating. This pageant is extremely popular in Salta.

Houses are generally built on plots of land of 10 meters by 25 meters separated from the pavement by a small garden. Houses have on one side a common wall and on the other a small garden.

The walls are of concrete blocks, plastered and painted. The roofs are constructed with prefabricated beams and hollow bricks, covered with colonial tiles.

They have an entrance porch, living-dining room, two bedrooms, bathroom, kitchen and a small washing area.

Most of the houses have been enlarged during the years by their owners (see Figure 50). The enlargements are not only due to the necessities of a larger family (increasing the number of bedrooms) but also by other types of

[1] Reported in: A. M. Battro and E. J. Ellis, "International Study of the Impact of Economic Development on the Spatial Environment of Children: Salta, Argentina," typescript, December 1972.

57
An aerial view of part
of Salta. Las Rosas is
at top center, between
the prison, the hills,
and the ruler-straight
major arterial with its
deep drainage ditch.
Note the triangular
plaza in the middle of
the community. The
city center is some
distance beyond the
lower left corner.

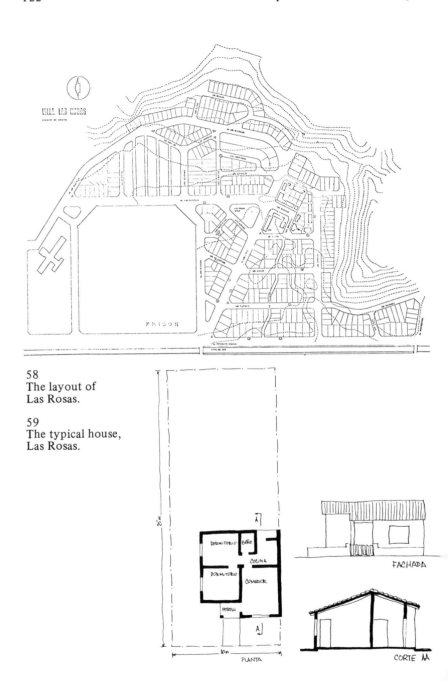

58
The layout of
Las Rosas.

59
The typical house,
Las Rosas.

necessities according to their way of living, such as enlarging the kitchen to provide eating facilities; setting up outdoor spots covered or half covered for small workshops, eating, clothes washing, etc.

The materials used for these enlargements are usually masonry walls or pillars and electroplated tin roofs. For semicovered areas, vined pergolas are used.

Houses were not fenced onto the street. Each owner could choose his type of fence and its construction.

There are many varieties of these, wire screens, with or without hedges, complicated forms and combinations of materials, bricks, stones, bricks or stones with iron railings, in some cases extending the porches until they reach the fences, built with materials or vined pergolas. The inhabitants of this suburb give a great deal of importance to the fence as it is the first impression of the outside of their homes.

There was one house with seven rooms, two with six rooms, and seventeen with five rooms, generally the enlargement of the kitchen does not constitute a new room. The type of construction is good. Only six houses can be considered well painted and with well kept gardens. Most of the houses are little cared for with objects heaped up in the living room (refrigerator, furniture, suits, mattresses, gramophones, TV, large tables, etc.). Apart from the useful objects, there is a large number of decorations and some religious images. [pages 16, 20, 26, 28, 30, and 59]

. . .

How would you describe your area to someone who does not know it, and who would like to know what it is like?

"It is a nice area, there are good friends, we have fun, we play."

"It is a nice area, big, it has a plaza, the Living Creche, the school, the hills, they are building a swimming pool."

"It is not very big, nice houses well decorated, flowers, trees, it has paved roads, there is a school, the plaza is a meeting place."

"Ample area, it is cool, nice hills and view. It is well protected because of the prison. I have many friends, and there is the Living Creche."

"It is a wonderful area, good, united neighbors. For Christmas we organize the Living Creche, I played the part of the dancing shepherd, we danced the 'carnavalito' [a local dance]. The plaza is good fun. The Local Neighbors' Organization is making a swimming pool."

"It is a nice area, many playful children, they play until late. The people are good. Many people go to the plaza at night. There are many birds in the hills."

"It is an amusing area, the girls organize parties, a Sports Club is being done. For the Christmas pageant I was an angel, and another year I was a shepherdess. People talk a lot about bad things, I don't like that."

"It is a nice big area, the neighbors are good. There is a plaza, a school, many streets and nearly all paved. During the Christmas pageant I was an angel twice and once a shepherd."

"It is a nice area, people come and go, cars pass, there are good buses. The plaza used to be nicer, better kept and with more flowers, some neighbours are good, others bad, there are many children."

"There is a model prison, the best in Salta, the prisoners work, they make chairs and bread and sell it to the public. Villa Las Rosas is a very nice, big area." [pages 39-40]

• • •

Are there beautiful places in your area or in the city and why are they beautiful?

"Within our area, the plaza and in the city the 9 de Julio plaza and the San Martin park, and the Guemes monument."

"The hills for picnics and playing."

"Monoblocks because there are many games."

"The plaza because I meet my friends."

"The Cathedral."

"I like everything in the city."

"The 9 de Julio plaza because it has lovely trees."

"The San Martin park because one can go for walks and it is always full of people."

"The plaza, because it is a happy place and there are always children playing."

"The Guemes monument, because we go there for picnics and there are lots of people."

"In our area the streets: Los Claveles [the carnations] and Las Magnolias [the magnolias] because there are pretty houses and paved roads."

"In the city the Cabildo because it is nice and is lit up at night."

"The street where I live, Los Tulipanes [the tulips] because there are many trees and the neighbours are very good."

"The hill, because that is nature."

"The front of my house, because there are always flowers."

"The San Martin park because everyone minds their own business."

"The National Shooting Range because you can shoot with firearms."

"The hill in springtime is like a green pillow."

"The 9 de Julio plaza is a cheerful place, many people go there."

Many answered "the grotto when they set up the Living Creche."

Only one child was pessimistic: "In our area there are no beautiful places."
[pages 50-51]

. . .

Do you think that [your children] are growing up in a better place than you
did?
     All parents agree that the present moment is favorable for the children, they
do not have to work, they study well, and they have a lot of freedom. Life in
general is less hard than before and the children receive all they need. Other
answers are the following:

"When I was my child's age, I used to work from sunrise to dusk, I lived in the
countryside. I had no bathroom, I earned one peso per day. Here in Salta there
are two social groups, you either are or you are not, life is very hard."

"Now the children have bicycles, movies, cokes, etc., everything that they
need and more."

"Before, education for girls was very poor and limited, only till second or third
grade."

"In my time we had much less freedom, everything was more difficult."

"I don't notice many changes."

"Before there was not such sociability among the children, different classes
were more divided."

"The same, when I was a child, we went through the same situation as now,
everything was expensive, salaries were never enough. There is unemployment,
many years will have to pass to be able to raise our children properly."

"Before, it was very hard to achieve anything, people had little chances."

"We were subjected to our parents' will, we had no freedom."

"University was impossible, now the State gives us more possibilities, also
economic."

"There exists more communication between parents and children."

"Women were sillier before and we had to work a lot." [pages 63-64]

. . .

In the following description, we will confine ourselves to the comments of
two children: Patricia (thirteen years) and Raul (twelve years) while we toured
together one of the most picturesque streets of the city: Caseros Street from
the 9 de Julio plaza up to the ancient San Bernardo convent. This segment of
the street is known for having some architectural monuments of real interest,
starting with the Cabildo on the Plaza, further on the San Francisco Church,
and ending with the San Bernardo convent that visually closes the street two
blocks from the church. Furthermore, the perspective of the San Bernardo hill
emerging like a huge triangular bulk behind the convent, gives a special touch

60
Scenes along the walk
in Caseros Street (a,
b, and d look east to
the San Bernardo hill,
and c looks to the
west).

a

c

b

d

e

f

g

to this road which is highly recommended as a traditional promenade of the city. Some old big colonial houses are still standing, for example: what today is the Uriburu Museum and some entrance halls, help one to imagine cool, flowered perfumed patios. The majestic wall of the San Francisco church and the many coloured facades constitute a landmark for a pedestrian tour. Notwithstanding, Caseros street has unfortunately lost its architectural unity and part of its quality during the last years.

Many old fashioned houses have disappeared, making way for modern buildings, most of them deplorable. The advertisements and signs, the aerial telephone and light wires, the parked cars, the bad conditions of the facades of many traditional houses, the shops with their windows totally out of tune with the surroundings, the lack of trees, the noisy traffic, just to mention the most obvious defects, certainly do not help to enhance the quality of this street which has been deteriorating noticeably.

Cars
"What I don't like is that the cars are allowed to park."

Sidewalks
"The sidewalks are too narrow and if a car comes one can be run down."

"Well, until they finish this building, it is bothersome for the pedestrians."

Trees and Gardens
"Here on the plaza of the Convent I would make a small garden. Here the stones do not bother. I would take the stones not in use, and use them to make a central flowerbed. Roses, daisies, carnations, two eucalyptus. If the sidewalks would be wider, yes, I would put trees, but if we widen the sidewalks, the roads get narrower."

Light and Telephone Wires
"The wires should pass somewhere else, it also makes it look bad."

"I don't think they bother."

"I think they bother, not because of the wires but because they make the church look ugly."

"Round the convent they bother me, cars park there, and light posts bother when you want to take photos."

"I would put the light wires underground."

Signs
"I don't like them, look at that one, it is not painted properly, it would need repainting."

"That acrylic sign, yes, I like, because it is well painted and at night it is easily seen."

Paint

"That the church is not painted, doesn't look well."

"Exactly, it looks bad."

"I don't like that corner either, because it is ruined, I would make them put better paint."

"I would paint the old signs, yes, those stuck on the wall."

"That yellow colour, I like it, because it is an old colour and the convent is old, but that cream yellow is sad and I don't like it."

"To fit this house, one should remove the top bars, take out the doors that it has, they are horrible, and paint the wall a peach pink colour."

"Yes, I like this convent, because it is well painted and well kept."

Antiqueness of the Houses

"I don't like this house because it is made of adobe [dry mud], and the other houses are made of bricks. Where this house stands, I would erect a building. This house should be repaired. The old ones I would demolish. This one, and that one on the corner."

"Yes, the corner house is horrible, if I would demolish a house I would throw down this one, and that one, well, I don't like it, it is too old."

"Well, the others I would leave them, because they are well finished, the stone one."

"I don't like that old house, it has staircases that are not used any more."

"In Salta, it would be better to demolish the old houses, because on repairing them the foundations would be too weak and they could fall."

Cleanliness

"I like everything in this block."

"This block is perfect."

"The City Hall would have to put something for garbage, because look at the streets and the sidewalks!"

View

"These houses bother me. . . . I would make a building and a park . . . a tall shopping center with seven floors. No, it wouldn't look bad next to the church, if it would cover the hill, I would do it all the same, because you see it perfectly well from here."

Movement

"The street I most like is Caseros, because of that curve it has."

"The view that I most sincerely like, is this one because it is ample." (Bells chime)

"Well, it is perfect, the street does not have any bad circulation, it doesn't have commercial signs, but I don't like it because it is too townlike, that one does not have any circulation, it seems desolate."

Design

"What I like about this house is the door, with its special design."

"Yes, I would like it very much that we have more houses like that one."

From these comments, we can see that the children are interested particularly in something that could be named "neatness," tidiness. A beautiful street must be a street with wide sidewalks, well painted facades, clean and with modern houses. Everything that looks untidy, such as wires, rickety doors, worn steps, deteriorated signs, old adobe houses, must be eliminated. This does not mean that the child does not know the aesthetic value of the ancient convent, he would even "like to live there" if it were a private house, but what most attracts his attention is the recent coat of paint that distinguishes it from other antique houses semi-abandoned or converted into cheap grocery stores. They prefer the noisy commercial street to the quiet residential one, they give a great deal of importance to luminous signs, in short, they value many aspects that they do not have in their area. On the other hand, the natural view (the hill) the plants and gardens that they see everyday in their area do not attract them majorly. They repeat an opinion, surely overheard from grownups, that in the center of the city there should be no trees, because they are dirty. It is as though they would attribute the word "dirty" to anything natural or wild, and the word "clean" to cement and luminous signs. In another city with other planning, for example Mendoza, where trees are found precisely in the city, at the edge of the irrigation channels, and not further out in the semi-desert surroundings, the child possibly would answer differently (for example, "outside the city you cannot plant trees, because there is no water"). [pages 88, 90, 91, 93, 94, 95]

· · ·

The test to be done is the following: the child is seated at a table in the school garden, facing the area's plaza. The experimenter asks him to draw the way that he has to go to reach the 9 de Julio plaza in the center of the city (about thirty blocks). The course has three changes of direction, A, B and C.

The result obtained confirms the hypothesis that we are dealing with a Guttman scale: the children who can correctly solve the change in course C, the furthest away, can also solve the intermediate B, and those that can find correctly the change in course B, can correctly draw A, the nearest to starting point. (The reproducibility coefficient of the test is very satisfactory: $Cr = 0.96$.)

It is interesting to point out that the major landmarks along the way are identified correctly, even though the change in course was wrong. This would lead us to believe that for many children of this age, the drawing of the way is of a topological kind and not necessarily euclidean (maintaining angles and distances).

In short, the children that we have observed, even though they know perfectly how to reach the center. of the city, have the most difficulty in drawing the last change of course (C). The difficulty increases as the change occurs further away from school. [pages 101, 107]

• • •

Poland

The work in Poland was more extensive, covering five groups of twenty to thirty children each: one group living in a center-city neighborhood and another in a peripheral housing project in both Warsaw and Cracow, and an additional group of rural village children in the Cracow region. The work, completed in 1974, was under the general supervision of Prof. Tadeusz Tomaszewski.[1] The Cracow studies were carried out by Prof. Maria Susułowska and Dr. Maria Sawicka; those in Warsaw by Prof. Tomaszewski, Dr. Andrzej Eliasz, Dr. Krystyna Skarzynska, and Dr. Teresa Szustrowa.

The Notion of the Quality of the Environment
The purpose of the research on perception of the environment, is to distinguish those properties of the environment which make the latter a "good" or a "bad" one for man. The research should above all yield information useful for town planners, organizers of the spatial environment in which people live. The information could be used in order to improve the quality of the environment. It could be useful for the organizers of the cultural life and educators as well, because both the quality of life and perception depend not only on properties of the environment, but also on those of a man. The quality of life in an environment should be created and improved from both these points of view simultaneously.

At the moment the research on the quality of life, quality of environment, and perception of the latter is in the initial stage, but the knowledge already existing allows us to formulate some preliminary theoretical and methodological assumptions for this type of research.

The difficulty in defining the notion of "quality of the environment" is connected with the fact that one's environment may be "good" or "bad" to

[1] Reported in: T. Tomaszewski, "Child's Perception of the Environment; UNESCO Project Realized in Poland, 1973-1974," typescript.

him in various respects. The following three aspects seem to be essential there:

First, the human environment, being the area of his vital activity, may influence that activity either positively or negatively. The activity of a man depends on his environment in three ways:

a. The environment is a pattern of sensory stimulation, a more or less organized source of stimuli, which determine one's activity level. From this point of view a differentiation should be made between optimal stimulation, stimulative deprivation and stimulative overload. According to rather common, but insufficiently supported views, the rural environment often provides situations of stimulative deprivation, while the urban environment creates situations of stimulative overload.

b. The environment is an area of the vital and behavioral activity of man, and from this point of view it is a system of elements meaningful to him. According to Kurt Lewin, it is a field of values and possibilities. Certain elements of the environment have for man the value of either goals or objects of avoidance; besides they may be regarded as means, i.e., factors either facilitating achievement of goals or making it more difficult.

c. The environment is an area of interpersonal relations, a space in which people meet, communicate, make acquaintances, cooperate, conflict, enjoy a good reputation, or are ill reputed, etc. Interpersonal relations and contacts may either be directly modified by the spatial organization of the environment (as by distance, neighborhood, dwelling in the same place, walking the same streets, etc.) or indirectly, mediated by a similar type of activity (waiting for a bus, going for a walk with children or dogs, entertainment in the same places, etc.).

Second, the environment is an area of the physical and mental development of man. It influences not only his physical and mental health, but also the process of forming his needs, views and opinions, his way of life, attitudes and strategies. It may organize or disorganize his personality, accelerate or retard his mental development, form his emotional life and be the source of his hopes and fears, activation, or discouragement. On this subject there are some commonly held opinions, not verified scientifically: for instance, the conviction that a rural environment is more favorable to the development of creative personalities than an environment of a great city, while the latter is said to be rather in favour of a highly determined routine.

The problem of the influence of the environment on human development is of special importance to planners. They must take into account that their spatial designs not only fulfill existing needs but also create new ones, and therefore their work, while satisfying people today, may not be satisfactory for them tomorrow.

Third, environment is a source of satisfaction or dissatisfaction for man, of his actual well-being or malaise. In one environment people feel comfortable and in the other the contrary: they approve of one while they disapprove of the other. Many planners consider that the subjective satisfaction of the user is their most important task.

But a differentiation should be made between active and passive satisfaction. Passive satisfaction, being of a static character, results from adapting the environment to the present needs of the individuals. Such satisfaction can be found in individuals living in very primitive conditions, with a minimal level of activity (a *far niente* satisfaction), or even within processes of physical or mental degradation (e.g., the satisfaction of alcoholics or drug addicts). Active and creative satisfaction, resulting from a high level of activity and development, is to be distinguished from this, the satisfaction of people participating in the development of their environment. The question arises whether it is possible to create spatial conditions favorable for this higher type of satisfaction by means of appropriate planning of the manmade environment.

Different environments may fulfill these three requirements of quality to different degrees. In the best case all three dimensions are at a high level, and in the worst case at a low level, respectively. Theoretically, there are numerous possible patterns between the extreme poles, e.g., there may be an environment technically underdeveloped, whose inhabitants are satisfied because the degree of their own development is rather low, their needs are small, and they do not know of other possibilities. There also may be an environment which highly activates people, not towards their development but their degradation.

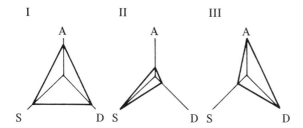

61
The three dimensions of environmental quality: A, encourages activity; D, supports development; S, gives satisfaction.

Diagram I represents an environment of a multidimensional high quality, one that activates, develops and satisfies people. Diagram II represents an environment in which people are satisfied, but inactive and underdeveloped. Diagram III represents an environment activating and developing people at the cost of great subjective effort and little immediate satisfaction.

Such theoretical constructs may be multiplied and probably each environmental structure has a corresponding characteristic pattern. Unfortunately, we do not yet have any appropriate empirical investigations." [pages 163-168]

• • •

The Cracow Region
The subjects of the city center group inhabit a narrow locality of the city, at the edge of the Planty. Kleparski Square is the central point of this locality (see Figure 6). In summer it is a market for vegetables and fruits, in winter,

mostly for meat and dairy products. The market square is rather chaotically covered with wooden stalls in which products are sold, either bought from suburban fruit and vegetable growers, or grown on in the traders' own farms. Although the market square is paved, the surface is usually covered with mud in the winter and dust in summer, and is littered with rotting vegetables and fruit. From early morning to late afternoon the place is very noisy and overcrowded, with hundreds of women shopping and chattering over price, pushing their way through congested narrow streets between the stalls. Numerous shops are situated in the buildings surrounding the market, i.e., a dress shop, a shop selling household goods, a delicatessen, a grocery, a self-service bar, and a restaurant of inferior sort, dirty and full of drunkards. On the opposite side of the market square there is the school of our subjects. The school building faces the market, and has neither a playground nor any other recreational base. The school children spend their school breaks in the overcrowded and busy market place.

A passage over ten meters wide leads from Kleparski Square to Basztowa Street, an artery of communication, through which lead the routes of four tram and three bus lines. The passage leading from the market square ends almost exactly at the point where the bus and tram stops are located. Thus the place is continually overcrowded with people going to or returning from shopping. In the same place are the offices of the Polish Airlines (LOT); their buses to and from the airport are parked on the edge of Kleparski Square, several meters further on, where Basztowa Street crosses Długa Street. Two tram lines ply along the latter street. From this crossing Slawkowska Street runs for several hundred meters to the Rynek, i.e., to the central square which is at the city centre. As Basztowa Street leads from the main railway station to this above crossing, the crowds are enlarged by the visitors following that route to the city centre.

The streets adjoining Kleparski Square are narrow, and dirty. Some of them are badly lit. Buildings in this locality are gloomy and shabby, originating mostly from the nineteenth century. Previously spacious apartments, occupying whole floors of these buildings, have been divided into a number of flats. The flats usually consist of one or two rooms, spacious (the average floor area ranges from 30 to 50 square meters), but not functional, and comfortless. Sanitation and water supply are often common to all the inhabitants of the floor, since it was originally designed only for one family.

In this region of the city centre there is no greenery, except for the belt of the Planty. The other exception is a garden adjoining the St. Philip Church. Children living in the neighborhood are allowed by the priests to play in the garden. No entertainment is offered to the young people in this locality, except for a youth club in the Railwaymen's House, in the neighborhood of Kleparski Square, and a police organized club for maladjusted adolescents. This situation may be compensated for by the nearness of the old-town district, which is the entertainment and cultural centre.

The locality selected for the suburban research is called "Na Kozłowce" or "Kozłowka" (see Figure 8). It is one of the newest districts of Cracow, situated near the road leading from Cracow to Zakopane, about 8 kilometers in straight line from the city centre. The first block of flats was built in 1967, i.e. almost six years ago. At present the district comprises sixty 5-storey blocks of flats (containing 75 flats each), and three 11-storey high rise blocks. The helical distribution of the detached blocks may give an impression of some chaos to persons accustomed to non-detached, rectangularly arranged buildings.

There are two categories of blocks and flats: so-called council houses and those of the housing cooperative. The former include all the houses built before World War II and some of the newly built buildings. These are the property of the State, represented by an appropriate governing authority. These flats are rented to people whose income is not high enough to allow them to participate in a housing cooperative. Therefore, the new council houses are intended for low-income families, whose living conditions have been poor hitherto (e.g., living in overcrowded flats, unsanitary conditions, etc.). These are built from funds provided by the State. The housing cooperative blocks are built with money paid beforehand by their future inhabitants, members of the cooperative, whose income is appropriately high.

There is no difference in construction between the two categories of blocks. The comfortable apartments are provided with central heating, gas, and sanitation, although they are rather small: a typical flat, containing two rooms, a bathroom, a kitchen and a little hall, has a floor area of about 36 to 40 square meters. Although the constructional plans are identical, there are some differences between the two types of blocks, mostly in details of finish and of the building site. The council buildings were erected in a hurry, as a result of the national housing shortage. This is reflected in the crude appearance of the blocks. They are left unpargetted, while the builders rush on to do their next tasks—leaving rubble, unfilled ditches and trampled earth behind them. The housing cooperative builders work more slowly, but more carefully, and so they leave clean, colourfully pargetted buildings, surrounded with lawns and young trees, and with paved pathways. These differences of finishing details can be found in all the newly built districts, as well as in Kozłowka.

During the six years of its existence the locality has been provided with a number of shops and a service system. At present, there are four groceries, one fishmonger's, one butcher's, and one greengrocer's shop. Besides, there are: a post office, a health service centre, a chemist's shop, a laundry, an establishment hiring out household equipment, an electrotechnical shop, a bookshop, and a library. A restaurant and a cafe were established some time ago, as well as so called "Practical Lady" shop, which offers the services of a hairdresser, a tailor and a cosmetician. A school and a nursery were opened as soon as first blocks of flats had been finished. These proved to be insufficient, so an additional elementary school and a nursery had to be built as the locality developed. A children's playground was established last year for the youngest inhabitants of the area.

At present, the population of the locality amounts to 16,000 persons. The council houses are inhabited by 5,000 people while 11,000 live in the housing cooperative buildings. About 70 percent of the inhabitants of the Kozłowka locality lived in Cracow beforehand, while 30 percent were employed in Cracow, but lived elsewhere.

Building operations are still being carried out, planned to be completed in 1975. At present the area looks depressing, partially because of the building operations. Besides, the identical blocks of flats, seemingly chaotically distributed in the open space, create an impression of monotony and boredom. The lack of courtyards, resulting from the use of detached buildings, makes the dustbins (which are not emptied frequently enough) together with scraps of building material, look most conspicuous in the open space between blocks. The majority of the young trees planted in the locality have been broken, and the lawns are trampled by the adolescents, who saunter idly about, and try to pick a quarrel with passersby. This seems to be a result of boredom, since there is no entertainment available. It takes at least thirty-five minutes to get to the city by one of four buses or two tram lines, which prevents everyday visits to the city centre.

A medium-size village, Bystra Podhalanska, was selected for the rural research, as a representative example of the villages in the Cracow province (see Figure 9). Bystra Podhalanska is situated in the mountain range of Beskid Wysoki, about 22 kilometers from Babia Mountain. The village is neither a popular holiday resort, nor are there any hostels and boarding houses. Therefore, urban influences are small and result almost entirely from the migration of young people to industrial towns in order to enter an employment.

Bystra Podhalanska has an area of 16 square kilometers and is surrounded by forests, mostly coniferous. The village is on the river Skawa and its tributary stream, the Bystrzanka. The topography is mountainous.

An asphalt road runs through Bystra Podhalanska, leading to the adjoining villages, Toporzysko, Olszyna and Osielec, and to the neighboring town, Jordanow. At the edge of the village is the local railway station. In addition, there is a bus line serving the adjacent villages and the three nearest towns: Jordanow, Makow Podhalanski and Sucha Beskidzka.

Brick buildings prevail in the village, and the number of old wooden houses is gradually decreasing. The rate of development can be illustrated by the fact that eight houses (out of the total number of 476) were built in the last two years. Moreover, a gradual modernization of the older buildings can be observed, since plumbing and sanitation are being installed. About 50 percent of the houses have running water, and in about 20 percent there are bathrooms and toilets. The village was supplied with electric lights in 1958, together with other Polish villages. At present most of the village houses have various electric devices, including radio and TV sets.

The village is of agricultural character and has a resident population of 2,343 persons. There are 488 separate farms, mostly small (up to 2 hectares in area). Farming is the only source of income for 20 percent of the population. The others have additional sources of income, mostly from employment in the Village Cooperative, in the Agricultural Cooperative, in factories outside the village area, and in the Polish Railroads. Besides, a considerable number of farms are engaged in the production of woodwork, on the domestic system. About 20 percent of the population are white-collar workers: teachers, medical staff of the health service centre, and functionaries of the Forest Inspectorate, etc.

The following State institutions and enterprises are in the village: a saw mill, a purchasing centre of cattle for slaughter, an Agricultural Cooperative, a Village Cooperative, a bar, a club, a cafe, four groceries, a bakery, butcher's shop, a shop selling household ·goods, and a clothes shop, a library, and a mobile cinema. Besides, there are an infants' nursery, and a nursery school, the latter in two buildings. The other local institutions are: the local administration of the Commune Council, a Forest Inspectorate, a police station, a health service centre and an Agronomic Centre.

Bystra Podhalanska is proud of its places of interest, namely: an eighteenth-century residence of Prince Radziwill (presently occupied by the Forest Inspectorate), and some very old trees, among which is a 600-year-old lime tree. The other important functional points include a church and a cemetery, according to the traditional rural mentality.

Bystra Podhalanska is picturesquely situated. It is rapidly growing and well managed, in other words, a typical contemporary Polish village. The architectural style characteristic to the highlands is preserved even in the new, brick houses. This seems to indicate that there is a harmony between the technical progress and the traditional culture, which emphasizes the regional individuality of the village.   [pages 10-17]

· · ·

The children interviewed differed with respect to the degree of their knowledge of the surrounding areas. This seems to result from the confinement of their daily activities (particularly for the city centre and new district groups) to a small, neighboring area, which they seldom leave, except on special occasions. The children's small spatial range influences their knowledge about the environment in various ways. In the rural environment this makes for a very thorough penetration of the entire village area; in the city centre group this confines the children's knowledge to the Old City (i.e., the central part of Cracow), while in the new district, the knowledge of the city is rather poor and random.

The difference can be seen in comparing the global maps made by both the urban groups with the actual plan of Cracow. It is apparent that the spatial range known to the city centre children is smaller than that of the new district subjects, yet the city centre children's knowledge of the area structure is accurate. Their map has no blank spaces. In the new district group, the map consists of a number of "islands," loosely connected with each other. (See Figs. 36 and 40.)

The different degree of knowledge of the surrounding areas results in a varied capability for representing the entire city area schematically. Typical of the new district group is a spatial orientation based on a set of places or transport routes familiar to the child, while in both the city centre and village areas the spatial image of distant places is usually more general and systematic.

Children of the area with a low density of important objects and institutions (the village) usually distinguish all the latter as places important in the environment. In the area with a high density of important objects (i.e., the city centre), whole systems of important points are distinguished (i.e., important streets), or a selection of places particularly important for the subjects is made. The new district children, whose knowledge of the city is rather poor, usually distinguish in the latter mostly the places known from their own experience.

The places important for the village children are those connected with their daily activities, and are scattered all over the area. As these children's household chores are usually much more extensive than elsewhere, they participate in the community life and perceive all the important objects that determine both the village living standard and its social status.

In the new district, the perception of the important places of the city is based on the children's "festive" activity. Their image of the city has some "festive" features: they perceive it as a place of entertainment, attractive shopping, and sightseeing.

In the city centre, the important places are distinguished on the basis of both observation and information (i.e., a traditional picture of Cracow as a town of monuments and universities), as well as on the attractiveness of some objects for the subjects themselves (places of amusements and outdoor activities). [pages 92-94]

· · ·

In the table below the responses concerning favourite places are shown. The term "green areas" includes: a park, a sports field or meadow; while "places of amusement" refers to youth clubs and cinemas.

| Favourite Place | Frequency of responses | | | | | | | |
| | Village | | City Centre | | New District | | Total | |
	Girls	Boys	Girls	Boys	Girls	Boys	Girls	Boys
Own home	6	2	3	3	8	2	17	7
School	3	-	-	-	-	1	3	1
Green area	5	9	4	9	2	7	11	25
Street	-	-	1	2	2	2	3	4
A friend's home	-	3	3	-	3	1	6	4
Place of amusement	-	1	3	1	-	2	3	4
New place	1	-	-	-	-	-	1	-
None	-	-	1	-	-	-	1	-

Open space (playgrounds or the street) is mentioned most frequently as the favourite place, in all the groups. The fact that boys mention open space twice as frequently as girls may be explained either by the former's larger sense of security or their larger need for motorial games.

The second most favourite place in all the groups is the subject's own home. It seems to be preferred because it gives them a sense of personal freedom. This interpretation is supported by the fact that, both in the village and in the city centre, where the dwelling standard is relatively lower (in the village because of the large families, in the city centre because of the small flats), the subjects mention their own home twice less frequently than they mention the green areas. In the new district group, who have the best dwelling conditions, the subjects' own home is mentioned almost as frequently as is the open space. [pages 99-100]

. . .

The subjects had no sense of restriction to their spatial freedom: no cases of subjects forced to fight for place were found in any of the groups. All the subjects responded that the streets belong to everybody, to the public, and that there are no "nobody's" places in the area. The differences between groups are concerned solely with the sense of ownership. In the village, fifteen subjects (nine girls and six boys) perceive some place as belonging to them, while in the city centre only four subjects (one girl and three boys), and in the new district seven (five girls and two boys). The difference between the environments is highly significant ($X^2 = 11.249$, $P > 0.01$, df = 2). In the village they mentioned: the house, garden, or farmyard; in the urban group, a bookshelf, a desk, an armchair, or, at the most, a part of a room. It may be concluded that the sense of ownership is really a sense of responsibility for a place. The latter is most intense in the village group, which probably results from the children's participation in the work of their families. As they help their parents, they literally become "joint managers" of the house or a part of it. In the city centre, where the children have their specific mode of life, parallel to that of adults but not shared with them, the subjects are responsible for a tiny part of their home at the most, since the flats are so small. In the new district, the situation seems to be essentially similar (the children are maintained by their parents and are completely dependent on them), but the dwelling standard is better. [pages 104-105]

. . .

The subjects listed the following places in which they do not like to be:
- school—because there one has to learn, be attentive, sit still, being in danger of bad marks (13 responses)
- own home—when the child has to work or learn according to his parents' orders (11 cases)
- houses in which the child pays a visit with his parents (which is boring) (10 cases)

- places which must be passed through, but which are dangerous, as hooligans may be encountered there (10 cases)
- boring places, in which "nothing happens" (6 cases)
- shops where one has to wait in a queue (5 cases)
- busy streets, since it's difficult to move, and an accident may happen there (3 responses)
- a forest and a cemetery, being sad and gloomy places (3 responses)
- strange, little known places, since it is easy to lose one's way there (4 responses)
- a visit to a doctor since "it is always unpleasant" (4 cases) [page 107]

· · ·

A number of the subjects perceived no troublesome elements in their environment, while others named one or several disturbing ones. The data obtained are represented in the following table:

Elements of the Environment Which Disturb the Subjects	Frequency of Responses							
	Village		City Centre		New District		Total	
	Girls	Boys	Girls	Boys	Girls	Boys	Girls	Boys
None	10	8	2	4	3	2	15	14
Drunken people	2	3	3	-	2	2	7	5
Roads in bad condition	1	2	1	1	-	-	2	3
Intense traffic	-	-	5	6	-	-	5	6
Combustion gases	-	-	1	2	-	-	1	2
Dirty streets and buildings	-	-	4	3	-	-	4	3
Noise	-	-	1	2	2	3	3	5
Road construction	-	-	-	2	2	-	2	2
Lack of places of amusement	-	-	-	-	1	5	1	5
Badly supplied shops	-	-	-	-	3	3	3	3
Queues in shops	-	-	-	-	4	2	4	2
Breaks in the water supply	-	-	-	-	3	2	3	2
Overpopulation	-	-	-	-	2	3	2	3
Other	2	2	1	-	-	-	3	2

In the village, the number of subjects whose everyday life is not disturbed is over twice as large as that of children who perceive some troublesome elements in their environment.

Contrariwise, in the city centre the number of subjects disturbed by some environmental factor is almost four times larger than that of subjects making no complaint about their surroundings. In the new district group the number of subjects fully accepting their environment is five times smaller than that of the disturbed ones. The differences between the environments is significant (X^2 = 19,956, P > 0.01, df = 2).

In all the environments an aversion to drunken people is a common attitude. Except for that, the objects and events perceived as being disturbing obviously vary depending on the environment. In the rural environment, roads in bad condition (i.e., covered with dust or mud, depending on season, as only the main roads are asphalted) are perceived as the principal disturbance. In the city centre, the disturbances are pollution, traffic, and noise. In the new district, the obstacles result from an insufficient supply of the necessary services, and are also connected with a sense of overpopulation, which is interesting. The latter might be explained by the type of housing in the new district. One building usually contains seventy to eighty flats, while a traditional dwelling house in the city centre will contain fifteen to twenty flats. The cubage of the latter buildings is only about a third smaller than that of a new district block of flats. The different cubage per apartment results from both the height of the flats, and their floor area—both considerably smaller in the new buildings. Thus, the subjects of the new district have a greater sense of lack of room and of being overcrowded, than do the children of the city centre, although the latter's dwelling standard is much worse, and the general density of population is considerably larger there. [pages 114-116]

. . .

The specific changes which have occurred in the environment within the subjects' memory may be classified as follows:

Type of Change Perceived	Frequency of Responses							
	Village		City Centre		New District		Total	
	Girls	Boys	Girls	Boys	Girls	Boys	Girls	Boys
A build-up	35	34	10	7	37	37	82	78
An improvement	18	21	9	11	7	2	34	34
A deterioration	—	—	6	1	—	—	6	1
An increase in population density	—	—	1	—	2	1	3	1
None	—	—	3	3	—	—	3	3

As it appears from the data presented above, about a fifth of the subjects from the city centre do not perceive any changes in their environment, while the changes observed are not always for the better. [pages 119-120]

. . .

Almost all the respondents think that various changes are likely to happen in their environment within the next ten years. Only four subjects, in the city centre, believe that nothing will change.

The responses concerning expected change fall into similar categories as those referred to in perceived change, i.e., an expectation of an improvement (city renewal, modern and aesthetic housing, better transport system); or a build-up (of new buildings of various types); or a deterioration of the existing state. Moreover, a number of subjects expect an eradication of some elements (demolition of old buildings, prohibition or limitation of vehicular traffic). Distribution of responses concerning the expected changes is the following in the three environments:

Type of Change Expected	Frequency of Responses							
	Village		City Centre		New District		Total	
	Girls	Boys	Girls	Boys	Girls	Boys	Girls	Boys
An improvement	15	13	12	15	6	1	33	29
A build-up	24	31	3	5	32	33	59	69
An eradication	—	—	6	5	1	—	7	5
A deterioration	—	—	—	—	1	2	1	2
An increase of population	—	—	—	—	2	3	2	3
None	—	—	3	1	—	—	3	1

[pages 127-128]

. . .

Correlation coefficients between the expected and desired changes in the environment are as follows:

the village group   0.40
the city centre group   0.20
the new district group   0.97

The city centre children see almost no possibility of realizing their proposed changes. The area is hardly susceptible to change, being full of old, nondetached buildings. Being aware that in the rural areas efforts are concentrated mostly on the increase of the agricultural production, the village children perceive only a small chance that their desires may be realized. But the new district children are convinced of the reality of their propositions, since the buildup of their area has not yet been finished.

It may be that in the village and the city centre the children seem to regard their desires as mere reveries, expecting any changes in their environments to be consistent with those hitherto introduced. The new district children seem to indulge in wishful thinking, as they expect that the development of their area will change its direction according to their desires.

This interpretation of the data may be supported by the children's responses to the question as to how they would imagine other people's attitudes might be towards their proposed changes. In the city centre fourteen subjects out of twenty-five believe that a number of people (usually adults) would not be pleased with their changes. In the village, almost half of the subjects (i.e., twelve out of twenty-eight interviewed) share this opinion: they think that the changes they desire would meet with disagreement and resistance from drunkards, unwilling taxpayers, and conservatives who cling to tradition.

In the new district, only seven subjects out of thirty doubt that their proposed changes would be accepted by the adults. The remainder optimistically expect a general contentedness. [pages 132-134]

· · ·

When interviewed a number of children could not answer the question as to where they would live in the next ten years. However, the majority seemed to have rather precise plans concerning their future place of residence. Generally the subjects can be divided into those who expect to live in another city or village, and those who would like to move only to another part of the city or to another house:

| Expected Place of Residence | Frequency of Responses | | | | | | | |
| | Village | | City Centre | | New District | | Total | |
	Girls	Boys	Girls	Boys	Girls	Boys	Girls	Boys
The same	6	9	12	11	5	7	23	27
Another house	1	3	3	1	2	–	6	4
Another part of the city	–	–	–	1	1	4	1	5
Another village	–	–	–	–	2	4	2	4
Another city	6	3	–	–	–	–	6	3
Don't know	2	1	–	1	5	–	7	2

The city centre children do not expect a change of residence; most often they wish to live in the same place. Any possible change would consist in a move to houses built in the period between the two wars, as these flats are both comfortable and spacious. Considering the very low dwelling standard of the majority of the children, their apparent disinclination to change their abode can be explained either because the area is so attractive that it compensates for the lack of comfort in the flats, or that the extremely small area of the flats in any new housing is perceived as being worse than the lack of modern conveniences in their present spacious flats.

Two-thirds of the children of the village area expect to live in their village in the future; some of them plan to live in a new house they are going to build for themselves. About a third of them wish to migrate to the city (mostly girls) in order to find an attractive job. All the children are going to continue their studies after primary school, mostly in secondary technical schools. Most of them expect to remain afterwards in the village, finding an occupation either there, or in one of the nearby villages. As it is much more difficult for girls with a secondary education to get an appropriate job in a village, it is understandable that it is mostly girls who expect they will have to move to the city.

In the new district, under a half of the interviewed subjects expect to live in the same place. The remainder either plan to move to houses with larger apartments, or (more often) to other, older parts of the city, or even to the countryside.

If the expressed desire to live in the same place in the future is an index of the children's acceptance of their area, it appears that the quality of housing conditions (i.e., the degree of modern conveniences and the number of persons in the flat) is inversely related to the degree of acceptance of the residential area. The new district children, who have the highest dwelling standard, least frequently expect to live in the same area in the future, while the children of the city centre and of the village more often wish to stay in their present habitation, although their living conditions are apparently much worse. The attractiveness of a place of residence may depend, among children, on the environmental opportunities of satisfying their physical needs (of playing, entertainment, freedom, security, etc.), rather than on their dwelling standard itself."
[pages 141-143]

· · ·

The children named different places when asked about the best place to live in, in contrast to when they described their future place of residence.

The following were mentioned as the best places to live in (with the reasons for the choice):
· countryside (30 responses)
   because of:
   fresh air (11)
   greenery (4)
   quiet (3)
   contact with people (3)

lack of vehicular traffic (3)
cleanliness (2)
open space (2)
a small number of people (2)
esthetic values (1)
· a villa in a suburban district (19 responses)
because of:
greenery (13)
fresh air (6)
the possibility of owning a swimming pool (6)
the right to own a house (4)
isolation from people (4)
lack of vehicular traffic (4)
quiet (3)
· the city centre (19 responses)
because of:
the nearness of all important places (8)
convenient shopping (5)
monuments (4)
entertainments (4)
the comfort of living (3)
traffic (2)
the opportunities of an interesting job (1)
· a new housing district (8 responses)
because of:
flats with several rooms (3)
spacious streets (2)
good lighting (2)
lawns (1)
· houses built in the period between the two wars (7 responses)
because of:
the solidity of the buildings (3)
the large flats (3)
soundproof flats (2)
lawns (2)
· a little town (4 responses)
because of:
fresh air (3)
the opportunities of getting a job (2)
houses larger than in the countryside (2)

Besides, nine children mentioned various places abroad: the Mediterranean coast received four responses; the United States, two responses; Tokyo, Paris, and Vienna, one response each. The children imagine the Mediterranean coast to be a land of evergreen trees, flowers in blossom, and sun. The United States is regarded as a country of high incomes and of technical progress. Tokyo, Paris, and Vienna were described as "beautiful cities," as the subjects had been told so by their parents.

The frequency of response concerning the best place to live was as follows for the particular study areas:

Best Place to Live In	Frequency of Response							
	Village		City Centre		New District		Total	
	Girls	Boys	Girls	Boys	Girls	Boys	Girls	Boys
The countryside	8	10	-	5	2	5	10	20
A suburban villa	-	-	5	2	6	6	11	8
The city center	4	3	3	5	2	2	9	10
A new housing district	-	-	4	-	2	2	6	2
Interwar housing	-	-	3	3	1	-	4	3
A little town	3	1	-	-	-	-	3	1
Abroad	-	1	-	-	6	2	6	3

[pages 143-145]

. . .

The groups were homogeneous with regard to their intellectual development, the social and economic status of their parents, and the accessibility of mass media. All the children were attending elementary schools with the same program, all of them were getting some extraschool forms of education and were travelling in the country. None of the village children has ever been abroad, thence they knew a little less of various urbanistic environments. This difference seems to be insignificant, however, as the urban children have had only short trips to bordering countries.

The interviewed groups differ with respect to their modes of life, particularly the extent of their duties. In the urban area practically the only requirement imposed on the children by their parents consisted in receiving good marks at school. Only infrequently the subjects (mostly girls) were asked to do some household chores (cleaning up, help at cooking, etc.). In the rural area, the children regardless of sex were considerably more burdened with duties, as they had to help in farm work, besides their school lessons.

In all the study areas, the children were granted a considerable personal freedom: restrictions imposed by the adults were few, and practically did not limit the children's possibilities of penetration of their environments. In the rural area the restrictions are imposed to prevent the children from any negative influences (contacts with alcoholics, or persons behaving improperly), while in urban areas limitations are concerned with the children's personal security (prevention from road accidents, hooligans, etc.).

The degree of parental control is different in the various environments, being relatively high in the village (where the parents mostly perform their work at home); considerably smaller in the city centre area (parents work out of home); and slight in the new district (parents waste much time in the journeys to work).

Differences between the areas were also found with respect to the children's dwelling standard: rather high in the new district, average in the village, and very poor in the city centre area. These differences seem to result from the degree of development of the environment. In the rural area, development is average, which allows some renewal and rebuilding. In the new district, almost all modern housing requirements are met, while in the city centre no radical renewal is possible, as the area is highly built up. The housing standards of the last century are still in force there.

The children's time budgets are influenced both by their dwelling standard and by the degree of parental control. In the urban environment where the adults are absent from home for the better part of the day (the new district) or where the children share the same room with the adults (the city centre), an "empty time" appears in the time budgets. This "empty time" is spent without any particular occupation. No such time can be found among the village children, as they are able to specify their occupations in almost every minute of the day.

In the city centre, the children's knowledge of both the nearest and surrounding areas is based on information supplemented by the subject's experience acquired from their daily and "festive" activities. The children go out of the nearby area infrequently, as all their needs may be satisfied there. Therefore, their maps of the whole city usually represent a precise plan of their local area, slightly enlarged by some other streets.

The rural area children gather their knowledge of the environment mostly by means of their daily activities, and information received from the adults. Their "festive" activities usually take place beyond the area, in the neighboring villages. The latter have similar function for the village children as that of the city for the new district subjects.

The new district children's knowledge of their environment is considerably differentiated, i.e., they know very well their own area by means of their daily activity, while the city centre is rather unfamiliar to them, being known partially by means of "festive" activities and partially through the mass media. Maps of the whole city drawn by these children correctly represent their own district, while the rest of the city is confined to a small fragment along the transport route they use to get to the city centre.

The groups differ also with respect to places considered to be functionally important. In the rural area all the distinguishable points (shops, bus stops, offices) are regarded as important ones. All public facilities and services are mentioned frequently, being considered to be symbols of social status.

In the city centre, fewer places were distinguished. Their importance was determined by the perception of the adults (to whom monuments and relic buildings are important), as well as by the children's own activities (places of amusement and outdoor activity).

In the new district, both types of perception were found: the children mentioned as important all the distinguishable places in their local area (shops, houses, infants' nurseries, etc.), while in their image of the whole city places connected with their "festive" activities prevailed (places of amusement, monuments, attractive shops).

The village children regard the various public facilities to be the most typical elements of their area, as they determine the village status. These children describe their environment as beautiful, perceive no restrictions imposed upon their activity, and almost no dangers (except for natural ones).

Buildings of historic character, heavy traffic, noise, and pollution are considered to be typical of the city centre area. The children feel endangered by the intense vehicular traffic, but the social dangers (particularly from drunken men) are perceived more often. The city centre subjects' attitude toward their area seems to be an ambivalent one: they describe the latter as beautiful, but dirty and noisy. The children emphasize the lack of greenery and places suitable for open-air activity.

In the new district, modern blocks of flats are most frequently mentioned as typical of the area. The children indicate no sign of acceptance of their environment: they have no sense of freedom, and perceive a lack of amusements, places for open-air games, and greenery. Besides, they feel the area is overpopulated.

The children's attitude towards their environment is also revealed in their plans for the future. The rural area children usually wish to remain in their village, and so do the city centre subjects. The new district children for the most part want to change their place of residence, preferably to a villa or to a village house.

Children of all the environments, in describing the best place to live in, mention such features as planting, fresh air, convenient transport routes to shopping and entertainment centers, and large, comfortable flats. These ideal features are reflected in environmental changes described by the children.

In both urban groups the basic desired changes consist of: a reorganization of the transport system, to allow greater personal security and to eliminate noise and air pollution; the planting of many trees; and the establishment of recreational and sports centers. The latter is mentioned as frequently as transport reorganization. In the new district area, an additional desired change frequently suggested is to provide the district with places of amusement.

In the urban groups, the children show an admiration for monuments and buildings of historic value. This admiration is expressed in frequent plans of renewal for the Old City district, of restoration of its old-fashioned character by means of substituting horse-drawn cabs for the vehicular traffic and the introduction of gas lighting in the streets.

For the village children a further development of public services and facilities is most desirable, as well as a further increase of the village status.

Generally it can be said that the children positively evaluate the buildup of housing, facilities, and services, now taking place in postwar Poland. The children expect further development. Those living in a less built up area believe that the direction of progress will be consistent with their needs. In a highly built up city centre area, the children are rather skeptical about their desires. They consider that their realization will not be possible in the nearest future.

No essential differences were found between boys and girls as far as perception of and feelings toward their environments are concerned. An exception consisted in the boys paying more attention to places of amusement and open air activities. This may result from their larger amount of leisure time than that of girls. [pages 154-161]

· · ·

The Warsaw Region

The first group of subjects lives in Powisle, an elongated district situated on the left bank of the Vistula, between two bridges: the Poniatowski Bridge and the Slasko-Dabrowski Bridge (see Figure 4). The district is bounded on the east by the river, and on the west by a steep escarpment, separating Powisle from the city centre. Formerly, the escarpment used to be a very distinct dividing line between this area and the rest of the town. With development of transport and the buildings now located on the escarpment itself, this division is gradually declining. However, Powisle still remains rather isolated.

Powisle is an old Warsaw district, with attached, dense, and rather chaotic housing. In distinction to other districts of Warsaw, many buildings here survived the war. These are mostly tenement houses, two to six storeys high. Formerly it was a poor district, inhabited mostly by craftsmen and small shopkeepers; presently the occupations and living standards of the inhabitants is much more differentiated. There are a few high blocks of flats built recently among the old houses.

The district is sufficiently provided with shops, repair shops, and other services, but it lacks cultural and recreational centers. There is no space for playgrounds or sportsfields in the traditional, congested housing. The access to the open areas, which are gradually being transformed for recreation, is rather complicated; it requires crossing busy streets with heavy traffic, as these green areas are situated immediately at the river side, across the bridge on the other side of the Vistula.

The district included in the research is in the neighborhood of Solec and Dobra streets, and of the Poniatowski Bridge and the railway bridge. In this area, the local traffic is enlarged by a busy artery of communication running along the Vistula. Moreover, the viaduct of Poniatowski Bridge is a part of the town's central artery of east to west communication, including several tram and bus lines. In the rush hour the intensity of traffic amounts here to 4,400 vehicles per hour (1973 data).

In the houses in the neighborhood of this viaduct the intensity of noise is estimated about 96 db when the windows are opened and 90 db when closed.

A considerable source of noise is the tram line on the viaduct. There is a regulation limiting the speed of the trams to 30 km/hour (which reduces the noise intensity to 78 db with windows closed). But it is not exactly observed, The other source of noise is the railway viaduct, which leads across the river close to the Poniatowski Bridge (the distance between the two viaducts ranges from 100 to 250 meters). Long-distance and suburban shuttle trains speed through the viaduct every several minutes.

Zatrasie is the second urban area selected for the research in Warsaw (see Figure 7). Within the capital, it is the most extreme contradiction to the Powisle district. Zatrasie is entirely new, laid out in 1967-1968 in an open space, according to carefully designed plans. It is a "model district," the result of a search for an optimal architectural solution. In architectural publications, it has been mentioned as an example of an excellent project, in opposition to "stone deserts" or "concrete uniforms."

The Zatrasie district is situated about 5 kilometers from the city centre, in a suburban area. It occupies the site enclosed by the triangle of Broniewski, Krasinski, and Elblaska streets, and is a closed urban unit, with its own system of shops and services. There are several convenient bus and tram lines, which allow one to get to the city centre in fifteen to twenty minutes.

Buildings in the district are various, from two to eight storeys high, arranged around a central square. There are numerous walks, playgrounds, sport fields, and green areas, but little free space. Some houses have small individual gardens, owned by inhabitants of the ground floor.

Much attention was paid to the problem of noise. There is no traffic within the district; garages and parking, as well as bus and tram lines, are situated on the periphery of the district. Therefore the intensity of noise is very low. [pages 180-183]

. . .

The Zatrasie children sleep an hour longer, spend a little more time on studying (the difference is insignificant) and an hour less on recreation, as compared with the Powisle subjects.

Recreational activities are less diversified among the Zatrasie children than among Powisle ones, as expressed in terms of the number of various activities mentioned by the subjects (78 versus 88, respectively).

Recreational activities are less specific in case of the Zatrasie children (they seem to engage in more "messing around" in their spare time), while in Powisle area the children more frequently indicate some special interests, such as pursuing a hobby. The difference is expressed in the proportion of 13 to 33 percent, respectively.

Recreational activities in Zatrasie are more frequently individual, and informal, while in Powisle they are more organized and formal (in a special interests school, a youth club, or a sport club, etc.). The difference is ex-

pressed in the percent of time spent in formally organized recreational activities, 2.5 to 11 percent, respectively.
No differences were found in the way of spending time on Sundays and holidays. These activities are generally organized by the children's families, and are similar in all the groups.
The following relations were found between the children's mode of life and their personality type:
* The children living in an environment adequate to their individual personality, i.e., in an area which provides them with the level of stimulation appropriate to their type of reactivity, spend more time on studying than the children for whom the environment is inadequate: 9.9 hours per week versus 7.5.
* The children who are understimulated (i.e., the ones who have a low reactivity level and live in the quiet district of Zatrasie) sleep longer than the other subjects: 9.8 hours versus 8.7 hours per day.
* The overstimulated children, i.e., the highly reactive ones, who live in the area offering a strong stimulation (i.e., Powisle), spend less time on studying and more on recreational activities than any other subjects. This is expressed by the proportions: 7.7 hours per week versus 9.1 hours, and 6.3 hours versus 5.3. [pages 208-210]

. . .

Perception of Zatrasie by Its Children
1. The routine activity area is closed within the district boundaries.
2. Open space is frequently mentioned as a benefit of the environment.
3. The locality is perceived as a separate unit; no relations with the rest of the town are perceived.
4. The environment is not perceived as noisy.
5. The environment is perceived as a rather unvarying one; any changes are for the better.
6. The functional image of the environment is less differentiated. Dwelling houses are the prevailing element.
7. The functional benefits of the environment are connected with the children's needs.
8. There is a weak sense of any limitation of activity.
9. An identification with the area.
10. A strong sense of security.
11. The children do not perceive their locality in the terms: interesting-uninteresting.

Perception of Powisle by Its Children
1. The routine activity area is not determined by any objective boundaries.
2. Open space is seldom mentioned as an advantage of the environment.
3. The locality is perceived in relation to other districts. Nearness to the city centre is regarded as a merit.

4. The environment is perceived as noisy.
5. The environment is perceived as changeable. Although it is generally improving somewhat, there are also changes for the worse.
6. The functional image of the environment is differentiated. The prevailing elements are of varied functions.
7. The functional benefits of the environment do not pertain to children's activities exclusively.
8. There is a stronger sense of limitation of activity.
9. A lack of identification with the area.
10. A weaker sense of security.
11. The environment is perceived as an interesting one.

In the light of the data, the preliminary assumption that Zatrasie is an environment beneficial for the activity and development of children living there, while Powisle is disadvantageous, seems to be controversial.

The children's manner of perceiving the two environments has revealed some other important features of the environment (besides the level of stimulation and the magnitude of open space), which are apparently connected with activity and development.

The differentiation between "closed" and "open" environments seems to be significant. The open environments facilitate expansion and hence enrich and individualize the experiences of children. Closed, isolated environments make expansion difficult, thus limiting and homogenizing experience.

At the same time, a sense of connection with the environment, which may lead to action for the latter's benefit, seems to develop more easily in a closed and small area. Such an identification is more difficult in open environments.

The functional differentiation of the environment is another important characteristic. A functionally differentiated environment, like an open one, enriches experience. In this respect Powisle is of better "quality" than Zatrasie.

The functional content of an environment seems to be equally significant. The more the functional qualities of environment correspond to the inhabitant's needs, the larger is the people's activity within the area, and the smaller their expansion beyond it.

As far as the needs of children aged thirteen to fourteen are concerned, both Zatrasie and Powisle have a number of important functions. Zatrasie offers open space designed for children, while Powisle supplies possibilities of contacts with culture, and open space as well, but the latter is rather distant from their dwellings, and not intended only for children.

Finally, the characterization of an environment in the dimension of secure-dangerous seems to be important. Powisle is apparently less secure than Zatrasie, which has no internal traffic. [pages 227-229]

. . .

In the "bad," old borough in the city centre, possessing few places in which children can spend their spare time, and plagued with intense traffic and noise,

the following comparisons can be made with the interpersonal contacts listed by children living in the "good," new, planned peripheral district:
* more names of persons known to the child were listed in the city centre district;
* a larger percent of persons were known who were outside of the child's school, family, dwelling place, or personal contacts;
* a larger percent of these contacts were based on material principles, and were fortuitous;
* there was a stronger tendency to neutral or negative evaluations in these interpersonal relations.

Generally speaking, "centripetal" interpersonal relations were more pronounced in the "good" planned area, while in the "bad" old one "centrifugal" tendencies were more frequent. Besides, in the "good" district there were stronger tendencies to personal relations that were more durable and emotionally positive, while in the "bad" district there were tendencies to material, impersonal and fortuitous contacts, neutral or even negative emotionally. [page 242]

· · ·

A detailed analysis of the children's drawings of their actual environment and the desired changes to it, has shown that drawings may be a valuable technique in studying children's perception of the environment. The technique allows us to uncover the essential categories used in perception, as well as to make numerical comparisons between children of various environments, with regard to some both quantitative or qualitative aspects of their perception. Thus the technique may be useful for comparative studies.

In both the groups, the realistic spatial organization of the district prevails in the child's picture. In the Powisle drawings, the linear system and its derivatives dominate, as they correspond to the real layout of housing along the streets. In Zatrasie, either a closed system is found in the drawings, or they are chaotic. It seems that the traditional arrangement along the streets determines the children's perception and imagination more strongly than the modern, detached layout does. (See Figs. 33 and 37.)

Structural elements of the environment appear more often in the drawings of Zatrasie children than in Powisle group (in the proportion 299 to 236), while functional elements are more frequent among the Powisle children (in the proportion 198 to 134). In other words, the Powisle children perceive their district rather as an area of their life and activity, as a system of appropriate opportunities; while the Zatrasie children think of their habitation as a collection of houses.

The frequency of occurrence of the various functional elements in the drawings is different in the two environments. The picture of the existing state in Powisle is richer and more differentiated than in Zatrasie. The only exception are the opportunities for motorial games, which are actually larger in Zatrasie, in keeping with the town-planning intentions. In Zatrasie, the opportunities for motorial activity prevail over other forms of activity, particularly

cultural. As far as the children's cultural life is concerned, school plays the
main role in Zatrasie, while in Powisle it is only one of the factors in their
cultural life. [pages 168, 171-172]

. . .

Mexico

The studies in Mexico were conducted by students from the University of
Southern California, supervised by Dr. Tridib Banerjee. The work was sup-
ported by the Comité Mexicano del Hombre y la Biosfera (MAB) and the
Instituto de Desarollo Urbano y Regional of Toluca. The interviews were conducted by Edward Johnson, Dennis Kirshner, Michael Calzada, and Marianna
Krabacher. Twenty children, ten boys and ten girls, were interviewed in each
location: the Colonia Universidad in the provincial capital of Toluca, and
Colonia San Agustin in the municipality of Ecatepec, on the far outskirts of
Mexico City. The studies in Ecatepec were linked to a larger study of migration
into Mexico City. Both studies emphasized the differences of behavior and
perception between boys and girls. They were completed in 1975.

Toluca
Toluca is a metropolis consisting of an urban core and surrounding semi-rural
pueblos.[1] The total population of the municipality is 240,000 with 115,000
living within the urban core. Toluca is 64 kms west of Mexico City. At an ele-
vation at 2514 meters, it is the highest city in North America. The Las Cruces
Mountains separate Toluca from Mexico City to the east, and to the west, a
mountain ridge includes the Toluca volcano, a national park, which is the
highest point in the Republic of Mexico. The landscape within the city itself is
almost flat. The hilly Calvario Park is the only elevated area.
    The climate of Toluca is temperate. The winter months are dry, and the
summer months are humid with some amounts of rain falling almost daily.
The city of Toluca is divided into various colonias or neighborhoods. Colonia
Universidad is located at the south-central edge of the city, and is a stable
community. Many of the families have lived in the area fifteen or more years.
An elaborate fiesta is held annually in celebration of the patron saint of the
colonia.
    79 percent of the total usable land is in single family housing, most of
which is classified as being of "low" quality and "economical" construction.
The colonia is physically well defined, bordered on the east by a private club,
secondary school, and low density housing; on the west by a preparatory
school and extensive school sporting fields; on the south by a heavily traveled

[1] Reported in: E. J. Johnson and D. J. Kirschner, "Children's Perceptions of
the Environment: A Case Study in Toluca, Mexico," typescript, summer 1975.

arterial by-pass. The colonia is approximately two kilometers from the central core. It is an area which has undergone rapid change in the past four or five years, during which period electricity, drinking water, drainage facilities and sewers have been provided for the first time. A new primary school and an adjacent park were constructed, and streets which were nothing more than dirt roads have been paved and provided with sidewalks and curbs. Although the area has maintained its single family residential character, apartments have begun to appear and the density has increased to the point where there is now almost no vacant land available. The children are unanimous in their estimation that all of the changes have been for the better. [pages 7-12] (See Figs. 10 and 11.)

. . .

The boys' maps contained much broader descriptions of the colonia, illustrating areas that were actually located outside of it. They would repeatedly mention sports fields and schools since it was in these areas where they spent much of their unprogrammed time. One boy reported once playing soccer in one of these sports fields until four o'clock in the morning. The girls were much more limited in the range of items mentioned. Not only did they fail to expand the colonia as the boys did, but they also neglected some of the striking features within the colonia. What did receive much attention from the girls, were the houses and stores. Houses and stores were mentioned by the girls three times as often as by the boys.

The great majority of the children stated that their favorite place was somewhere outside of the colonia, such as Alameda Park, Calvario Park, the volcano, school, the movies, or the sports center. But the one area outside of the colonia which the children knew best was the central city. The girls referred to this area almost exclusively despite being asked to draw maps of the entire city. They identified such places as the portales, detailing the stores within them and naming the actual items sold there. They also took great care in drawing the zocalo area, devoting much attention to the palace buildings. The boys, on the other hand, did not concentrate as much on details of the centro. Their maps were broader in scope, with as many non-centro references as those to the centro itself. They mentioned the sports area, the University, the Plaza of Jaguars located near Calvario Park, the military base sports field, the bus terminal, and the new market, none of which were identified by the girls. When asked to write the names of places they knew within the city, this same pattern of identification emerged. The number of items located within the centro that girls identified was double the number that boys listed. The girls would mention the plaza, churches, banks, specific stores, schools, and markets while the boys spoke of things such as the social security building, museums, the centro, and Club Toluca—a private recreational area. The girls concentrated on detailed items, while the boys referred to the centro in general.

Despite the fact that girls concentrated on the centro when mapping, the range of items they identified and talked about during the interview was significantly broader. One of the areas they mentioned frequently was the Calvario, a hilltop park within which is located a museum, a church, a small zoo, and various gazebos. The park affords a beautiful view of the surroundings, and is one of the few green spaces within the city. Of all the places mentioned in maps and interviews, the Calvario was one of those referenced most often. Neither boys nor girls had any trouble correctly identifying photos of this area during the photo recognition test and it was the overwhelming choice of all the children when asked to identify pretty places within the city, even though other green spaces were also mentioned. [pages 15-22]

· · ·

The spontaneous mapping of the city, in view of the broad range of items from which one can choose, requires the area to be highly distinctive to the child in order to be identified. The interview questions, which restrict the range of possible responses, allow an area of less absolute distinction to be identified. The photos require the least amount of distinction for an area to be identified, since only a casual association is necessary for identification.

Referring to the data in Table 1 which shows collective responses for boys and girls, it can be seen that differences exist. For example, the boys consistently identified photos of the Calvario area, but only occasionally mentioned it during the interview session or drew it in their cognitive maps. The girls consistently identified the photos and occasionally mentioned it during free recall, but, in contrast to the boys, generally failed to make any reference to it in their maps.

With the exceptions of the centro, which everyone knew and the area on the eastern fringe of the city which no one knew, the intensity of the image the boys possess of the city seems to be only slightly stronger than that of the girls. Also, the geographical range of areas known to the girls appears to be

TABLE 1   Identity of Places

	Centro	Calvario Park	University Area	New Market	Tolucan Industrial Area
	P I M	P I M	P I M	P I M	P I M
Boys	Y Y Y	Y ? ?	Y ? ?	Y ? ?	? N N
Girls	Y Y Y	Y ? N	Y ? N	Y N N	? N N

Y = yes, a notable number knew the photo of the place, or a notable number mentioned the place, or a notable number drew the place on a map

N = no, a notable number did not know the photo of the place, or a notable number did not mention the place, or a notable number did not draw the place

? = the responses were mixed

M = drawn on the map

I = mentioned in the interview as a place they knew

P = recognized the photo

significantly beyond the home and stores. These are curious findings, contrary to the impression one gets after an examination of the maps and interview responses where the girls emphasize houses and stores. It also runs contrary to what one would expect of the lower class Mexican culture which requires the girls to remain immersed in the home environment. The evidence supports the hypothesis that the formerly restrictive culture is now permitting a larger range of environmental awareness for girls as well as boys. [pages 24-27]

. . .

The most obvious factor, observing the children draw their maps, was their continually recurring awareness of streets. They would usually begin by drawing a few streets, locating their house or school along the street, and then proceeding to locate other houses, stores, parks, schools, and playing fields in sequence, relative to the street and their house. When shifting attention to another street, they would turn the map to maintain their orientation along the street they were representing. It was as if they were mentally walking along, turning the map as they mentally turned the corner, and recording on the map what they saw as they traveled. (See Fig. 41.)

One part of the colonia which almost everyone neglected was the eastern street edge. This street was diagonal to all the rest and upset the grid-like pattern. The easternmost blocks were triangles or truncated triangles instead of squares or rectangles. Very few children attempted to represent this area, despite the fact that they repeatedly drew items that were located on either side of this street. The children would continue their gridiron and ignore this nonrectilinear intrusion. This nonsymmetrical area was the only point of spatial confusion within the colonia.

Within the zocalo are two government palaces directly across the plaza from each other. The architecture of these two buildings is almost exactly alike. One of these buildings, the Legislative Palace, contains a public library and has two fountains in front of it, while the other, the Palace of Justice, has neither. In their city maps the children repeatedly represented the Legislative Palace, calling it the library, and also mentioned it as an important building within the city. They neither drew nor mentioned the Palace of Justice. The similarity in appearance of the buildings was not enough to give them equal meaning. The fact that the children frequently used the library within the Legislative Palace and that it was near a unique physical landmark in the form of the fountain gave the Legislative Palace a special meaning.

When asked to identify important places, the children would generally mention buildings, in particular the governmental palaces. The children would explain "they are the center of government activities," you "pay bills at the government office," "it gets water for people," you go there to "take care of things," they are the places "where government lives and works." Banco Commercio was important because it is "big with lots of money and many people," the Blanco Department Store because you can "buy a lot," the portales because "there are more things there and it brings in tourism." These places are identified as important because of how they are used [pages 28-34] (See Fig. 42.)

. . .

The children spoke of moving to where they could get an advanced education or better job. But their future plans for careers reflected an optimism that was not supported by the statistics of the general census, for all the children spoke of continuing their education to a college degree. Careers in law, accounting, veterinary medicine, teaching, and science were mentioned, illustrating their aspirations. One child replied specifically that his career would be in "something that needs a lot of education." One senses a great pressure on the children to go to school, for education is seen by their working class parents as the only means for upward mobility.

Another area of similar response was the question of dangerous places. Most children felt that the traffic was the most dangerous characteristic of their environment. The responses of the parents were similar. A child would mention a particular traffic circle near the edge of the colonia and the parent would name the same circle during a separate interview.

The children felt a need to "improve housing of the poor," and to "provide more houses." One child was even willing to sacrifice Calvario Park because he felt the city "needs land for people" and "therefore [he] would put in more houses in its place." Children were aware of the modernization and urbanization which was occurring. They preferred modern two-story homes to more traditional colonial homes. They also spoke of the importance of owning a house. [pages 35-38]

. . .

The time-budget provided evidence of the importance of the child's role in the household management. It reveals a wide range of household duties which the children are expected to perform. They include cooking, washing, feeding the animals, gathering firewood, attending younger brothers and sisters, shopping, running errands of various sorts, and feeding adult members of the family. Most of these duties are performed by the girls, which leaves them little time for activities of their own choice. Discretionary activities are centered around their house or the houses of friends. Even playing in the parks is restricted.

Boys have more free time. They report spending most of their unprogrammed time in parks, sports fields, or going to the movies. As with the girls, it appears they lack the time to investigate the wild areas of Toluca: not many knew about the deep, wide, drainage ditch on the west side of town; there was no mention of going outside the city limits to agricultural open spaces. When shown pictures, the children expressed fears of danger within these areas, rather than interest in them as possible play areas. Also obvious is the absence of youth gang activities of any sort. There is virtually no mischievous crime in Toluca by gangs or individuals of any age. [pages 39-42]

. . .

Parks are mentioned many times, but that number declines as the use requirement implied in any given question increases, that is, in the series: pretty
places; favorite place; best place to be with friends; best place to be alone;
draw the places you know; what did you do yesterday. Green spaces are referred to almost exclusively, when naming "pretty places." The children mention Calvario nearly unanimously, Alameda, Zaragoza (a smaller park east of
the centro), the Marquesa (a national park located between Toluca and Mexico
City), the volcano, trees, playing fields, and the country in general. Green
spaces were also the overwhelming choice as favorite places. Parks are also
mentioned as the best place to be with friends, where again some children
would mention the same places that they identified as favorite places and
pretty places. But the majority of places referred to were areas that were used
more regularly, such as the neighborhood schools and libraries. [Moreover,
observation showed that the parks, although used, were not used heavily
enough to justify the amount of attention they were given in this question.]
When speaking of best place to be alone, the home was the place mentioned
most often. [pages 44-46]

· · ·

In some playing fields, permission must first be obtained to use them. Existing
green spaces are divided up with a specific use for each section, which is also
an effective deterrent to unprogrammed use. In many cases the spaces are
fenced off to discourage any use whatsoever. Trees are being planted, which
are sorely needed for visual relief, but they are either neglected or uprooted.

Traditionally, the streets have been a popular gathering place, utilized more
often than parks. They provide an excellent conduit for unprogrammed activities. But in Toluca the traffic is formidable: heavy and fierce on the main
streets, unpredictable and darting on the side streets. The danger is reflected in
the children's responses. They declare almost unanimously that this is one of
the primary factors they would change if they had the power. The children
not only considered this danger as a deterrent to playing in the streets but also
indicated that it limited their mobility. Unfortunately, the streets are becoming
more crowded while controls remain inadequate. This source of uncontrived
"action space" remains untapped.

A third traditional gathering place is the centro. However, while the centro
is an attraction for visiting, looking, and walking, it is not useful for gathering.
There are a few scattered billiard rooms and dance floors in town, but little else
where teenagers can hang out. There was a small storefront with pinball ma-
chines, but it did not maintain late hours and was not in business long. [pages
49-52]   · · ·

Some green areas had little effect as visual amenities. One such area is along
the Tollocan Highway to Mexico City, an industrial strip with large lots, land-
scaped with grass, shrubs, and fountains. In the photo recognition test most
children failed to recognize these areas. Occasionally, the children travel to

Mexico City via the Tollocan, so they have opportunities to see this green space while driving past it. In addition, when questioned about places they knew or liked, the children mentioned other places that were even further along the same Tollocan, to which they could not travel without passing these industrial areas they claimed not to know. The places they remembered were unstructured open spaces, available for everyone's use. The industrial areas were enclosed by fences and usually guarded. There is a park within the colonia, but it is very small with no trees. Half of the children didn't draw the park in their maps although they drew the adjacent school. Perhaps this invisibility is due to the restricted activities that could take place there (just as restricting fences blocked the image of industrial areas), and the contrived manner in which it is sectioned off. Parks should be designed to allow a variety of uses within their boundaries. In the colonia park, the principal activities are playing marbles or using the swings. True, the park was designed for younger children, but they, too, grow tired of marbles and swings all the time. [pages 63-68]

. . .

Throughout this study evidence suggested that the cultural environment of the Colonia Universidad children is changing. The girls, although still predominantly housebound, are knowledgeable of areas outside of the home environment and have almost as wide a wandering range as boys. They aspire to more than the traditional roles of mother and housewife and speak of technical or professional careers. The boys, meanwhile, have more time for discretionary activities than was traditionally the case. All the children are becoming aware of financial social and political forces and of the changing quality of the environment. They seem to be moving away from orientation around the home. [page 73]

. . .

The research associates were from outside the culture and knew Spanish only as a second language. As a result, the initial contact with the children in Toluca was through the schools. However, after several meetings a relaxed rapport was established, and the cultural differences did not appear to be a serious handicap. Children under twelve years of age had difficulty understanding the questions and articulating answers. Children over fourteen years of age were often found to be working full time to help support the family, with attitudes and values basically reflecting that status. Therefore, the final study groups consisted of ten boys and ten girls between the ages of twelve and fourteen years of age. To compensate for any latent language barriers, a series of nonverbal photo recognition tests were employed along with the interviews. These tests cross-checked the information regarding range and general knowledge of the city, architectural preferences, and attitudes about dangerous places. This procedure proved successful and provided valuable information which otherwise might have been lost. It is recommended that it be included within the core research techniques for all future studies of this nature. [pages 77-80]

Ecatepec

Ecatepec was founded on the shores of one of the once predominant lakes which form the north watershed of the La Sierra de Guadalupe.[1] Like all the lake settlements, it was involved in intensive intertribal warfare. In 1320 A.D. it was integrated into the Aztec dominions. Cortez took possession in 1527. He passed it on to a daughter of Moctezuma II, she having married the Spaniard, Juan Paz. Throughout all the colonial period Ecatepec was a stop-over for viceroys before entering Mexico City. Mexico's hero, José Maria Morelos y Pavon, was executed here. There are numerous other historical landmarks, museums and tourist attractions located in Ecatepec. As a result of its heritage six major celebrations are held in the months of June, July, August, and September.

In 1960, Ecatepec had a population of 40,815, and reached 216,408 in 1970. A census taken in 1973 estimates 700,000 inhabitants. Ecatepec extends north from Mexico City and the Federal District, and occupies an area of 55 square miles, 9300 feet above sea level. The climate is subhumid temperate, with rains predominantly in the summer. Ecatepec survived primarily on subsistence agriculture until 1946 when the governor established a tax for industrial development. Ecatepec, being in the area zoned for development, began to flourish and presently there are 600 industrial installations there. The growing community of San Agustin lies within this municipality, situated on two-thirds square miles of the dry bed of the dying lake, barren and sterile. San Agustin was laid out on a grid, but the grid has a distinct axial direction due to the greediness of land developers who could thereby sell more land per lot. The narrower north-south streets limit vehicular traffic, and the accessibility of services (electric power lines, water trucks, trash pick-up) is also constrained by this, which thus becomes a primary concern of the inhabitants. Public transport service to and from the area is also limited. (See Figs. 12 and 13.)

. . .

The girls were interested in the schools for academic reasons mainly, while the boys mentioned schools with the playgrounds in mind. All of the girls considered the market an important place, when only one-half of the boys thought so. The boys knew specific routes and street names, while the girls seemed to have only a general knowledge of main avenues. Lastly, the girls mentioned their own home or a friend's home as important places more than the boys. The boys were very familiar with the surrounding communities of San Agustin while the girls seldom mentioned these colonias. The girls seemed to romanticize their worlds, alluding to dreams or hopes of visiting places they had seen or had heard about. The boys were perhaps more realistic. [pages 3-5]

. . .

[1] Reported in: M. F. Calzada and M. Krabacher, "The Environment and Child Perception," and "The Environmental Perceptions of Adolescent Boys and Girls, San Agustin, Ecatepec, Mexico," typescript, summer 1975.

We asked the adolescents if they could remember any changes in their area.
Again the girls indicated an interest in food and shopping by mentioning the
market. The boys listed street improvements above all. They use the streets for
soccer and other games. The young girls were seldom observed playing in the
streets. [page 5]

· · ·

The daily schedule question turned out to be very informative. The girls tend
to sleep nine hours a day, the boys eight hours. The girls tend towards eating
three meals a day, spending 2.5-3 hours to do so. In contrast, the boys eat
mostly two meals a day, spending only 1.5-2 hours in eating. School times
averaged to four hours a day for both sexes, but study times were different.
Girls spent a median of 2.5 hours per day on homework, and boys 1.75 hours.
The outdoor activities of girls occupied a median of 2.25 hours per day, while
boys' outdoor hours were 4.25 hours as a median per day. The girls spend
3.5 hours a day doing chores and errands, while the boys spend only 1.75
hours. The boys' evenings were largely devoted to the outdoor activities until
approximately 9:00 p.m. Girls would not have the permission to be outside in
the evening, except with an escort. All of the young girls interviewed needed
to have permission to go places throughout the day. Boys needed to have permission to go places alone, but did not appear to be as sheltered by their
parents. [pages 5-6]

· · ·

Are there pretty places in San Agustin? Four boys and four girls simply said
"no." Other boys mentioned bordering colonias as having pretty tree areas.
Other girls tended to mention public places such as the market, church, and
playgrounds. Many of the interviewees would prefer to live in an area with
trees and open spaces. [pages 6-7]

· · ·

An additional question dealt with the aspirations of the children. All planned
to have professional careers which would demand a high level of educational
attainment. The low economic background of their parents will not allow
them in most cases to attain this goal. Nevertheless, these are their aspirations.
More than half of the girls hoped to become bilingual or executive secretaries.
Seven of the girls interviewed stated that they would not give up their careers
after marriage. The few responses from the males reflected the idea that work
is the responsibility of the husband. As for the girls, it appears that there is a
trend away from being "home-bound" like their mothers and grandmothers. At
least at this adolescent age the girls interviewed appeared to want to be a part
of the general trend towards women's liberation. [pages 7-8]

· · ·

There were many suggestions for improvement in San Agustin. The boys mentioned the need for more games for children, soccer fields, parks and gardens, superior schools (past secondary), buses, supermarkets, patrolmen, drinking water, crossings on the main avenue Lourdes. The girls appear more community conscious and humanitarian, listing similar responses, but adding even more suggestions for the benefit of the general community and those in need. For example: to give land to the poor; to help poor children go to school (and to help their parents financially); to build a community recreation center; traffic lights on highways; education for people to care for the parks and keep the streets clean; more government schools where one does not pay. [pages 8-9]

. . .

The most fascinating data collected proved to be the image maps drawn by the children. In general, the girls followed a number of patterns which were not characteristic on the boys' maps. In many cases there was a focus on the home. The homes of the girls and their friends were often made distinguishable among the others, when boys' homes were depicted as a box or a simple lot with an X. Houses often had more detail, and even slanted roofs, which do not exist in San Agustin. In many cases the maps had affective or romantic qualities. There was a limited cognitive awareness. A girl would be familiar with her own concentric area but not with outlying areas. Girls would recognize the existence of a landmark, but would not know its exact location. Orientation was often inaccurate. Public services were more frequently labeled and depicted. Their own school was a focal point shown with much detail. The tortilleria and markets were often drawn in detail, with labels on individual stores. Streets were often left unlabeled, whereas the boys were very accurate and knowledgeable about street names and locations. Outlying areas were not labeled in most cases, except for the older girls of fifteen who traveled to the federal district daily. Their cognition of the environment proved to be very rich, and surprisingly different than that of the younger girls. (See Fig. 43.)

Distinctive characteristics of the male image maps were: to show the playing field as a central attraction; to include the bordering colonias; to underemphasize the private (home was seldom drawn in detail and was not distinct from other houses on their maps); to be aware of important landmarks, and to label them and most street names in detail. Their layout of the important places and streets was usually accurate, whereas the girls placed landmarks about where they belonged, or where they would fit into the scheme of the map. There were characteristics shared by the maps of both sexes. Most of the maps seem to "fade out" on the edges, as they reach unknown areas. The central business district is shown as the focal point of their daily lives. The main transportation routes (such as Lourdes Avenue) are predominant, and the east-west movement of traffic is emphasized while the north-south side streets are underplayed. The main east-west avenues make definite divisions of the colonia on most maps. [pages 9-12]

. . .

BIBLIOGRAPHY

Appleyard, Donald, and Lintell, Mark, "Environmental Quality of the City Street," *American Institute of Planners Journal* 38:2 (1972).

Bachelard, Gaston, *The Poetics of Space,* New York: Orion Press, 1964.

Barbichon, Guy, "Espace villageois, espace urbaine, dans l'imagerie enfantin," *Revue française de sociologie* 16:539-559 (1975).

Barker, Roger, "On the Nature of Environment," *Journal of Social Issues* 24:4 (1963).

Carr, Stephen, and Lynch, Kevin, "Where Learning Happens," *Daedalus,* Fall 1968.

Chombart de Lauwe, Marie-Jose, "Enfant-en-jeu," Paris: Centre nationale de la recherche scientifique, 1976.

Cobb, E., "The Ecology of Imagination in Childhood," *Daedalus* 88, 1959.

Coles, Robert, "What Poor Children Know about Buildings," *Connection,* Summer 1966.

Craik, Kenneth, "The Comprehension of the Everyday Physical Environment," *Journal of the American Institute of Planners* 34 (1968), pp. 29-37.

Demonstrativbauansnahmen des Bundesministeriums fur Städtebau und Wohnungswesen, "Kinder in Neuen Stadten," Bad Godesburg, 1970.

Draper, Patricia, "Crowding among Hunter-Gatherers: The !Kung Bushmen," *Science,* October 19, 1973.

Goffman, Ernest, *Behavior in Public Places,* Glencoe, Ill.: Free Press, 1963.

Golledge, Reginald, and Moore, Gary, *Environmental Knowing,* Stroudsburg, Penn.: Dowden, Hutchinson, and Ross, 1976.

Goodey, Brian, "A Checklist of Sources on Environmental Perception," Centre for Urban and Regional Studies, University of Birmingham, Research Memo No. 11, 1972.

———, "Images of Place; Essays on Environmental Perception, Communications, and Education," Centre for Urban and Regional Studies, University of Birmingham, 1974.

Grey, Arthur, et al., *People and Downtown,* Seattle: University of Washington Press, September 1970.

Harrison, John, and Sarre, Philip, "Personal Construct Theory in the Measurement of Environmental Images," *Environment and Behavior* 3:4 (1971).

Hart, Roger, "The Child's Landscape in a New England Town," Ph.D. thesis, Clark University, Department of Geography, Worcester, Mass., 1976.

Klackenberg, G., "The Development of Children in a Swedish Urban Community," *Acta paediatrica scand.,* suppl. vol. 187 (1968), pp. 105-121.

Ladd, Florence, "Black Youths View Their Environments," *Journal of the American Institute of Planners* 38 (1972), pp. 108-116.

Lowenthal, David, and Riel, M., "Publications in Environmental Perception," (8 vols.), New York: American Geographical Society, 1972.

Lukashok, Alvin, and Lynch, Kevin, "Some Childhood Memories of the City," *Journal of the American Institute of Planners* 22:3 (1956).

Lynch, Kevin, *The Image of the City*, Cambridge, Mass.: The MIT Press, 1960.

——, "The Openness of Open Space," in *Arts of the Environment*, Gyorgy Kepes, ed., New York: Braziller, 1972.

Maurer, Robert, and Baxter, James, "Images of the Neighborhood and City Among Black, Anglo, and Mexican-American Children," *Environment and Behavior* 4:4 (1972).

Moore, Robin, "An Experiment in Playground Design," MCP Thesis, Department of Urban Studies and Planning, MIT, 1967.

Parr, A. E., "The Child in the City: Urbanity and the Urban Scene," *Landscape*, Spring 1967.

Piaget, Jean, *The Child's Conception of the World*, London: Routledge and Kegan Paul, 1929.

Proshansky, Harold; Ittelson, William; and Rivlin, Leanne, *Environmental Psychology*, New York: Holt Rinehart, 1970.

Rapoport, Amos, "Observations Regarding Man-Environment Studies," *Man/ Environment Systems*, January 1970.

Sommer, Robert, *Personal Space*, Englewood Cliffs, N.J.: Prentice-Hall, 1969.

Southworth, Michael, "An Urban Service for Children Based on an Analysis of Cambridgeport Boys' Conception and Use of the City," Ph.D. thesis, Department of Urban Studies and Planning, MIT, 1970.

Spivack, Mayer, "The Landscape of Fantasy and the Real Live Playground," paper presented to the American Ortho-Psychiatric Association, Washington, D.C., March 1967.

Stea, David, and Downs, Roger, "From the Outside Looking in at the Inside Looking Out," *Environment and Behavior* 2 (1970), pp. 3-12.

[to which may be added many perceptive novels, children's stories, and memoirs of childhood]

Index